# THE GREATER EXODUS

## MONTE W. JUDAH

Published by Talmidim Publishing
Norman, Oklahoma

Cover design by Ephraim Judah

Lion and Lamb Ministries
PO Box 720968
Norman, Oklahoma, 73070-4752
www.lionlamb.net
(405) 447-4429

Copyright © 2013 by Monte W. Judah

ISBN: 978-0-9745269-9-7

The Greater Exodus
Eschatology, Bible, Messianic

All rights reserved. Except for brief excerpts used in review, no portion of this text may be reproduced or published with the expressed written permission for the author or the author's agent.

First Edition, 2013
Printed and bound in the United States of America
**Paragon Press**
**3029 South Ann Arbor Avenue, Oklahoma City, Oklahoma 73179 USA**
paragonpress@coxinet.net, 405-681-5757

# TABLE OF CONTENTS

Acknowledgements.................................................................v
Dedication.........................................................................vii
Foreword............................................................................ix

1. God Planned the First Exodus ...........................................1
2. God Has Planned for Another Exodus ..............................9
3. How Does God Save all Israel?........................................17
4. Having Eyes to See and Ears to Hear .............................25
5. Why Judaism Believes in the Greater Exodus...............35
6. Ending the Exile and Working Toward Restoration.......47
7. The Great Tribulation and the Greater Exodus..............61
8. Who Is Able to Stand in that Day?..................................73
9. Comparing the Future with the Ancient Past.................87
10. How Judaism Prepares for the Greater Exodus............105
11. How Messianics Prepare for the Greater Exodus.........119
12. The Two Houses of Israel in the Greater Exodus.........131
13. Transitioning to Tribes in the Camp..............................145
14. The Cloud by Day, the Fire by Night.............................157
15. Coming Face to Face with Him......................................171

A Diary into the Future......................................................181
Tribulation Timeline............................................................188
Index of Scriptures.............................................................190

# ACKNOWLEDGEMENTS

I want to thank my wife Lin, who has been my life companion and teammate in my ministry. Having been born on a former Feast of Tabernacles, she has shared the destiny of this message every bit as much as Sarah, Rebekah, Leah, and Rachel did for the Fathers.

I also want to express my appreciation of the staff of Lion and Lamb Ministries. None of them have been paid adequately for their professionalism and skill. Nonetheless, they have endeavored to spread my teaching to multitudes. In particular, I want to thank Jane Greene for her skill and assistance in editing and production of the manuscript; Lorne Greene, David Addington, and David Laredo for their counsel in the revision process; and my son Ephraim Judah for his invaluable layout and graphic design of the manuscript. Finally, I want to thank the Lord for His leading in my life. If this text is received well, then the credit is His. If there is error found, then that was my part.

# DEDICATION

The older generation in the Egyptian exodus balked when they were about to enter the promised land. They feared the inhabitants of the land would harm them and their children. As a result, they refused God's promise and were judged in the wilderness. The LORD then led their children into the land. I dedicate this book to my children and grandchildren with the prayer that they will complete the *Greater Exodus* with strength and courage. Remember what the LORD said to Joshua with a slight edit.

> *No man will be able to stand before you all the days of your life. Just as I have been with Moses, I will be with you; I will not fail you or forsake you. Be strong and courageous, <u>for you shall be the people who will possess the land which I swore to your fathers to give you</u>. Only be strong and very courageous; be careful to do according to all the law which Moses My servant commanded you; do not turn from it to the right or to the left, so that you may have success wherever you go.* **Joshua 1:5-7**
>
> *Have I not commanded you? Be strong and courageous! Do not tremble or be dismayed, for the LORD your God is with you wherever you go.* **Joshua 1:9**

# FOREWORD
## WRITING A BOOK AND CHOOSING A TITLE...

I had the privilege of meeting and speaking with Dr. Herbert Lockyer, Sr. before he passed away. He was the author of *All the Men of the Bible*, *All the Women of the Bible*, and another fourteen books cataloging a variety of topics about the Bible. He shared with me that he did not begin writing until he was 65 years of age. He was 94 years old at that time.

I was struck by how he only wrote about what he had studied all of his life and simply compiled lists using a steno pad and his personal Bible—a book with the covers torn away, now bound by yellowing Scotch tape and assorted Bible maps. Normally, a guy begins retirement at age 65; however, Dr. Lockyer was starting his life as an author.

I contacted Dr. Lockyer because of his treatise on the Book of Revelation called *Drama of the Ages*. He was genuinely excited that I had read his book. I wanted to ask him about his commentary on the 144,000 described in Chapter seven of Revelations. He believed and strongly argued for a very literal exegesis of that passage, that the day would come when the children of Israel would be distinguished as tribes again (not just as Jews). I agreed with that point and I sought more evidence to justify it.

When we finished our conversation, I walked away with a new perspective for my life and possible future. I am now 64 years of age, and the time has come for me to do what Dr. Lockyer showed me was possible; however, I am not writing this with

# FOREWORD

a steno pad. I have a nice computer and a large screen to read my text. My Bible, though, is similar. The back spine has come loose and the cover flops around like a fish out of water. I have used duct tape rather than Scotch tape to hold many of the sections together. The silver sheen of the tape is much better than the yellowing of old glue. Like Dr. Lockyer, I can't find anything in those other nice Bibles I have. I know where every verse is in mine. Dr. Lockyer also lamented that there was no end of writing books. I don't see any reason why my lot will be different.

The subject of this book is a topic I have taught in my public ministry for many years as a Messianic believer. There are not many teachers who fully embrace or try to advance the topic along with me. When it comes to the subject of the *end times*, topics such as the rapture and what happens to the United States in the future dominate the public arena. For various reasons, still others simply don't want to read or hear what the prophets of Israel said.

I am hopeful that this text will change that and bring insight to many. Most evangelical believers and all Messianics I know believe that the return of the Jews to the land of Israel is prophetically significant. In our generation, we have seen the ancient words of the prophets of Israel come alive. The modern state of Israel is a living testimony to the fact that there is a God of Israel. In every struggle with their neighbors, we are taken back to an ancient struggle between Jacob and Esau. We see the words of Zechariah (Zechariah 12:2-7) that Jerusalem has become the center of controversy and Judah is a firepot among sheaves (surrounding nations). But, beyond those words, God has promised to bring back all the scattered of Israel and every one of the remnant from the remotest parts of the earth. The modern state of Israel today is only the down payment upon a much more extensive prophecy.

# FOREWORD

Jeremiah said that the day was coming when we would say the word *exodus* and it would not be about the ancient Egyptian exodus. Instead, he said we would refer to something far more significant, far more profound, and far more dramatic for the world. He said God would bring all of His believers (native and alien) to His land, there they would worship Him together at Mount Zion.

In teaching this subject, I have sought to title it for ease of remembrance. Inspired by Jeremiah's comparison, I call it *The Greater Exodus*.

ONE

# GOD PLANNED THE FIRST EXODUS

Most of us know the story of the Egyptian exodus either from prior teachings, your own Scripture reading, or from the movie *The Ten Commandments*. Despite those sources, you probably did not hear about the prophetic implications for the end of the ages. To understand that, let's review the Egyptian exodus. The purpose in the plan for the Egyptian exodus is the same for the *Greater Exodus*.

Many believers think that God's primary purpose in the Egyptian exodus was to save Israel from slavery, that it was a story of freedom. If that were so, why didn't God just blind the Egyptians while Israel escaped, or for that matter, why didn't God slaughter the Egyptians heralding a great military victory for Israel and the oppressed? God could have done that. He did that at Jericho. But God had a very specific purpose in bringing Israel out of Egypt in the way He did. He wanted the Egyptians, the children of Israel, and all the people of the world to know the LORD. He was fulfilling promises made to our fathers Abraham, Isaac, and Jacob by laying a foundation for the redemption by the Messiah, and setting the stage for the end of the ages.

He wanted the world to follow the One True God instead of following false gods. Here is the first description of God's plan for the exodus which He gave to Abram (called Abraham after his son Isaac was born):

> *God said to Abram, "Know for certain that your descendants will be strangers in a land that is not theirs, where they will be enslaved and oppressed four hundred years. But I will also judge the nation whom they will serve; and afterward they will come out with many possessions. As for you, you shall go to your fathers in peace; you shall be buried at a good old age. Then in the fourth generation they shall return here, for the iniquity of the Amorite is not yet complete."* **Genesis 15:13-16**

Not only did God prophesy to Abram about the Egyptian exodus, He also hinted about how He would use the exodus from Egypt to judge the Amorites. Sure enough, when Moses and the children of Israel came out of Egypt, (430 years to the day of that prophecy – *Exodus 12:41*) there came a time when Israel defeated the Amorites as a judgment from God upon them. This is a specific example of God planning and then working the plan to completion.

Following the prophecy, the Book of Genesis gives us the account of how Abraham then fathered two sons. The first was by Hagar, his wife's handmaid, and the second by his wife Sarah when she was beyond the age to bear children. Even though Abraham loved Ishmael, the boy was later sent away with his mother Hagar, because he was **not** the promised son by God and the descendant line of the prophecy. Abraham and Sarah did bring forth a son and named him Isaac, the promised son who married Rebekah, and she bore him two sons. They were twins, the firstborn was Esau, the second son was Jacob. Like Ishmael, Esau was not the descendant line of the prophecy, even though Isaac loved Esau. God prophesied to Rebekah while she was pregnant that the older Esau would serve the younger Jacob.

Jacob then married two sisters, Leah and Rachel, and fathered children through them and their two handmaids, Bilhah and Zilpah. Jacob fathered twelve sons and one daughter. God also gave him the name *Israel* as he returned to the promised land with his family. One of Jacob's sons was Joseph, the firstborn of Rachel, Jacob's beloved wife. The story of redemption then begins with Joseph being sent by his father to check on the welfare of his brothers. Joseph was scorned by his brothers and sold into slavery, resulting in his journey to Egypt. There he rose up literally from prison to become the Viceroy of Egypt. When the same brothers came to buy food because of a famine, Joseph acted on the prophetic dreams he had been given as a youth to bring about reconciliation with his entire family. This resulted in 70 descendants of Jacob moving down to Egypt where four generations would live. This is how Genesis sets the stage for the birth of Moses and the Egyptian exodus.

The story of the biblical fathers is also a compilation of troubles and difficulties, having suffered various wrongs and indignities, and coming to a climax in the fourth generation in Egypt. There, the descendants of Jacob suffered greatly at the hands of Pharaoh and his taskmasters. They were enslaved just as God had said.

Moses lived during that fourth generation, nearly suffering the loss of his own life at birth due to Pharaoh's decree against Hebrew male children. Moses was discovered hidden in the bulrushes and reeds of the Nile River by Pharaoh's daughter and was raised in Pharaoh's house. When Moses grew to manhood, he chose to stand with his Hebrew brethren and slew an Egyptian because he was harming a fellow Hebrew. Believing the matter to be known, Moses then fled to the land of Midian and became a shepherd for his father-in-law Yithro (a descendant of Ishmael commonly called Jethro). Then in fulfillment of God's promise to Abram, Moses encountered the God of his fathers at the burning bush. He was dispatched by God to return to Egypt and bring the children of Israel out of Egypt. But the exodus from Egypt was not just to deliver and save them out of Egypt. God had some definite purposes that went beyond the deliverance of Israel in those days.

God wanted Pharaoh and the Egyptians to know that He was the LORD and that the other gods they worshiped were **not**. He wanted them to believe and trust in Him—the One True God. He wanted the Israelites to know Him. He wanted other nations of the world to know Him, and He also wanted all of the resulting generations of the world to know of Him. This is why God poured out numerous judgments upon Egypt, each one was a judgment upon a god of Egypt. Each time Moses announced a judgment, he would explain that the LORD was the One True God, not the gods they were worshiping. The tenth judgment was the *Passover*, the death of the firstborn of Egypt and the protection of Israel's firstborn. The firstborn was considered to be the very strength of the nation and the people. Moses then commanded the children of Israel to commemorate the Passover and Feast of Unleavened Bread every year at the same time. The Passover was concurrent with the final judgment upon Egypt (the moment the children of Israel were redeemed out of slavery) and the Feast of Unleavened Bread came from the "bread of haste" which they ate as they escaped.

Let us consider this memorial commandment a little deeper. When the Passover seder (order) is kept, four ceremonial cups are used to teach the next generation (our children) the ancient story of what God purposed and planned in that exodus.

> *Say, therefore, to the sons of Israel, "I am the LORD, and I will bring you out from under the burdens of the Egyptians, and I will deliver you from their bondage. I will also redeem you with an outstretched arm and with great judgments. Then I will take you for My people, and I will be*

*your God; and you shall know that I am the LORD your God, who brought you out from under the burdens of the Egyptians. I will bring you to the land which I swore to give to Abraham, Isaac, and Jacob, and I will give it to you for a possession; I am the LORD."* **Exodus 6:6-8**

Even today, the four ceremonial cups of the Passover seder are sanctification, instruction, redemption, and praise. They model the four phrases: "I will bring you," "I will deliver you," "I will redeem you," and "I will take you for My people." But these four phrases are encased in the words "I am the LORD" at the beginning and at the end.

These same words encase and surround the plan for the *Greater Exodus*. It is also embedded in the first commandment of the Ten Commandments given to those who escaped Egypt. "I am the LORD your God who brought you out of the land of Egypt and out of the house of slavery!"

Why did God set up the Egyptian exodus and its resulting judgments? It was to teach everyone who the LORD was and to demonstrate the process of redemption by knowing Him. Yet it was only part of the redemptive plan. God's plan of redemption extends throughout all generations. The real punch line to God's purpose is manifested in the *Greater Exodus*. Truly, when God fulfills the *Greater Exodus* the whole world will know who the LORD is.

Simply said, there is a future Passover and a future exodus for us at the end of the ages. Moses led the exodus and he was the first to say that there would be a future exodus, as you will learn in this text. The Messiah spoke of it as well, connecting it to His return. The Jewish people refer to the future Passover and exodus as the "final redemption." Each year at the Passover seder, they look forward to the future redemption (the *Greater Exodus*) by setting a special cup for the prophet Elijah.

## GOD PLANNED THE FIRST EXODUS

Let us go back to the exodus to examine more of God's purposes. Why did God lead Israel into the wilderness? Why couldn't they just get on the road others used and travel right to the promised land? There are several answers to this, but the greatest one extends from God's purpose to be known by them. He led them to the mountains where Moses had been dispatched. This is where God gave His instructions to live by. God planned for the wilderness journey.

> *He humbled you and let you be hungry, and fed you with manna which you did not know, nor did your fathers know, that He might make you understand that man does not live by bread alone, but man lives by everything that proceeds out of the mouth of the LORD. Your clothing did not wear out on you, nor did your foot swell these forty years. Thus you are to know in your heart that the LORD your God was disciplining you just as a man disciplines his son.*
> **Deuteronomy 8:3-5**

In reality, the children of Israel did not know how to live with one another and in the presence of God. God needed to teach them how to live. To do that, He gave them His Torah (the teaching), which are the first five books of the Bible, also called the Law of Moses, so they could inherit and enjoy the promised land.

> *Therefore, you shall keep the commandments of the LORD your God, to walk in His ways and to fear Him. For the LORD your God is bringing you into a good land, a land of brooks of water, of fountains and springs, flowing forth in valleys and hills; a land of wheat and barley, of vines and fig trees and pomegranates, a land of olive oil and honey; a land where you shall eat food without scarcity, in which you shall not lack anything; a land whose stones are iron, and out of whose hills you can dig copper. When you have*

*eaten and are satisfied, you shall bless the* Lord *your God for the good land which He has given you.*
### *Deuteronomy 8:6-10*

The commandments of God (Torah) define life and how to live it. They define what is holy and profane, what is clean and unclean, what is pure and impure, what is sacred and what is common. They explain how to come near to God and how God comes near to us. The Torah defines the tabernacle of God and how God does the business of reconciliation and atonement. The Torah also defines the Messiah and how He will be the acceptable substitute sacrifice for willful, defiant sin worthy of death. He was killed as our sacrifice so that we will be passed from death to life.

If one were to summarize the entire Torah into a few sentences it might go like this. The Torah is the story of a generation of Hebrews and how God delivered them out of slavery, established them as a nation, and led them to His promised land. The first book, Genesis, simply explains where they came from and how they got stuck in Egypt to begin with.

Yet, the instruction of the Torah doesn't end there. Its final pages are a message from Moses to the final generation of the ages. Moses is the first teacher of the *Greater Exodus*.

Those who are part of the *Greater Exodus* will be part of a plan made by God. It will not be happenstance. They will depart at a future Passover, eating the "bread of haste." They will plunder the "Egypt" of wherever they are. They will go into the wilderness, not the path of normal travelers. They will be led by the Lord and be provided with the basics of life. It will be humbling and life-changing. When it is completed, they will join resurrected saints from all the ages and walk into the Messianic Kingdom, the true promised land.

**GOD PLANNED THE FIRST EXODUS**

**TWO**

# GOD HAS PLANNED FOR ANOTHER EXODUS

God has an incredible plan to deliver (save) His people at the end of the ages. It is not the rapture. It is not the rapture prior, during, or after the great tribulation. The rapture is part of the resurrection just before we inhabit the kingdom. Instead, God is going to lead His people out of their homes, form mobile camps, and lead them into the *wilderness of the peoples* (out of the cities of the world). I call it the *Greater Exodus*. It will be similar to how God delivered the children of Israel from Pharaoh and the Egyptians. In fact, the story of the ancient Egyptian exodus is also a prophecy of how the saints will be delivered at the end of the ages.

There is more prophecy in the Old Testament Scripture about the triumphant coming of the Messiah than there is about the actual events of Yeshua of Nazareth coming and doing the work of redemption as the "Lamb of God." Those Scriptures talk about a great tribulation with the Messiah returning on a white horse; it primarily details God's faithfulness to His people (the remnant of Israel) and how the Messiah will bring them back the exiles from the nations to live permanently in His promised land. In particular, it lays out the plan for how and when the remnant (those who remain, those who are left, and those who are the believers) will escape. It provides clues as to how they will survive in the world with the antimessiah trying to destroy the remnant, and it is direct and honest about how they will endure to the end while God judges His enemies.

However, not everyone will be delivered. The Scriptures define two other destinies. First is the "sword destiny." This destiny will be those who attempt to "stand their ground" with weapons (the sword). The LORD said, "Those who take up the sword will die by the sword." The second destiny is captivity. They will not escape, choosing to simply withdraw to their homes in the hope of outlasting the events. They will be arrested and taken captive. Then they will die after a short internment.

Yet, the believers who "escape, survive, and endure" will be delivered by following God's plan of dwelling in a sukkah. Allow me to define that word more thoroughly. A *sukkah* is a tent, booth, hut, or tabernacle. The modern day equivalent could be an RV, a travel trailer, a pop-up tent, truck camper, or a tent set-up on the ground. A sukkah is a temporary shelter place with *mobile* capability. The plural of sukkah is sukkot (alternate spelling is Succoth). Sukkot is also the Hebrew name for the Feast of Tabernacles/Booths, which takes place in the fall after Trumpets and Atonement. Throughout this treatise I will refer to "sukkot" and "tabernacles."

Those believers who go on the great journey escaping, surviving, and enduring will do so for three and a half years (approximately 42 months). They will be separate from all of the other peoples of the land and avoid the cities in whatever nation they are living. Their destiny will be to journey into the kingdom and see the return of the King of Glory.

History is prophecy that has already happened, and prophecy is history that has not yet happened. God has done this more than once for many prophecies in the Bible. For example, the story of Joseph being sent by his father Jacob to see to the welfare of the flock and his brthers is the beginning of the story of *redemption* in the Bible. In the course of that story, Joseph is rejected by his brothers, cast into a pit, lifted out of the pit and taken to Egypt as a slave. However, the next time his brothers see him, he is effectively in charge of the world and selling food in Egypt. This is the same story of redemption accomplished by Yeshua the Messiah. He was rejected by His countrymen, buried, raised from the grave, and went somewhere unknown, but there is a day coming when they will discover that this same Yeshua is King of the whole world. This is but one example of how the stories of the patriarchs are actually prophetic pictures of what happens to their descendants. The simplest teaching of prophecy by the Jews is "What happens to the fathers will happen to the descendants." This is re-enforced by the various teachings about God throughout the Bible. Isaiah said it very succinctly.

> *Remember this, and be assured; recall it to mind, you transgressors. Remember the former things long past, for I am God, and there is no other; I am God, and there is no one like Me, declaring the end from the beginning and from ancient times things which have not been done, Saying, "My purpose will be established, and I will accomplish all My good pleasure; calling a bird of prey from the east, the man of My purpose from a far country. Truly I have spoken; truly I will bring it to pass. I have planned it, surely I will do it."* **Isaiah 46:8-11**

God is not impulsive. He does not do things like a man, starting one thing and doing another. He plans and does what He says. This principle of God foreknowing and prophesying out of historical events is part of His very character and faithfulness. God does this purposefully to manifest Himself and to cause us to trust Him. How does this work for us personally? When we remember the things of the past and understand God's purposes, we then discover what God is doing with us at the end of the ages. God knows the details of the end and shares with us when we understand the beginning. Men start things and hope they work out. Men are considered clever if they can get unrelated events to work together. God considers every event to be related and works them out. Most importantly, God does what He plans. When a man plans something and then actually executes that plan to success, we call him brilliant and a great leader. This is the only way God works.

Given that we understand the true character of God, we should seek to understand His plan. Ignoring His plan and saying, "Well, God is going to do whatever He wants," is not following His instructions. He shared the plan with us, laid it out from the beginning, and emphasized it through His prophets so that we would believe in Him. To do otherwise is evidence of unbelief.

God's great plan for the end of the ages is told to us in the ancient story of the children of Israel coming out of Egypt, their journey through the wilderness, and their preparation to enter the promised land. His plan is embedded in His stated purposes for the Egyptian exodus and the specific events that took place. Simply said, the plan for the end is part of the story of the beginning. Consider this: God built a relationship with our fathers Abraham, Isaac, and Jacob. From the children of Jacob, He formed twelve tribes, which became a nation in captivity. He then demonstrated His redemption with a slaughtered lamb and brought them out of captivity. He gave laws and instructions to live together and live by. This nation then entered the land and was supposed to model the future Messianic kingdom. He brought forth the Messiah who does the work of redemption as the "Lamb of God" so that all of the families of the earth might be blessed. But Israel rejected this redemption and found themselves scattered throughout the nations of the world. The stage is now set for the end of the ages. History becomes prophecy. The very words of God have said it, *"Truly I have spoken; truly I will bring it to pass. I have planned it, surely I will do it."* God must bring back all of His people from the lands of His enemies as He promised Abraham and us, his descendants.

God's plan for the end of the ages is extensive. It is not embedded in a few verses. It is pervasive, extending from Moses and the original exodus story through the prophets to the words of the Apostles and the Book of Revelation. The great expectation of the Jewish people is that the Messiah will lead this exodus and use it to manifest Himself to the world. As you will see, the prophecy specifies that the people on that journey will say that the Messiah is leading them.

The Jewish people have been taught that the *Greater Exodus* will begin at a future Passover and once again the "bread of haste" will be eaten. They believe that it leads to keeping the Feast of Tabernacles as the first assembly in the Messianic kingdom.

The prophecies of Jeremiah make a very dramatic comparison of the Egyptian exodus to the *Greater Exodus*. Jeremiah essentially says that the *Greater Exodus* will overshadow the ancient one to the point that the very reference to the "exodus" will become the default definition for the *Greater Exodus*. You will have to specify the "Egyptian" exodus to converse about the previous event.

> *"Therefore behold, days are coming," declares the L*ORD*, "when it will no longer be said, 'As the L*ORD* lives, who brought up the sons of Israel out of the land of Egypt,' but, 'As the L*ORD* lives, who brought up the sons of Israel from the land of the north and from all the countries where He had banished them.' For I will restore them to their own land which I gave to their fathers."* **Jeremiah 16:14-15**

Jeremiah repeats this comparison and adds how the Messiah will lead the future exodus.

> *"Behold, the days are coming," declares the LORD, "When I shall raise up for David a righteous Branch; and He will reign as king and act wisely and do justice and righteousness in the land. In His days Judah will be saved, and Israel will dwell securely; and this is His name by which He will be called, 'The LORD our righteousness.' Therefore behold, the days are coming," declares the LORD, "when they will no longer say, 'As the LORD lives, who brought up the sons of Israel from the land of Egypt,' but, 'As the LORD lives, who brought up and led back the descendants of the household of Israel from the north land and from all the countries where I had driven them.' Then they will live on their own soil."* **Jeremiah 23:5-8**

Jeremiah summed up God's plan for the *Greater Exodus* with these words.

> *"For I know the plans that I have for you," declares the LORD, "plans for welfare and not for calamity to give you a future and a hope. Then you will call upon Me and come and pray to Me, and I will listen to you. You will seek Me and find Me when you search for Me with all your heart. I will be found by you," declares the LORD, "and I will restore your fortunes and will gather you from all the nations and from all the places where I have driven you," declares the LORD, "and I will bring you back to the place from where I sent you into exile."* **Jeremiah 29:11-14**

Jeremiah is not the only prophet to speak directly of the future gathering from all nations. Moses has much to say. In fact, Moses speaks of it quite dramatically. He refers to it in the beginning and at the end in the Book of Deuteronomy. He spoke first to warn his brethren to obey the Lord in the land, but knowing full well that they would falter and be scattered to all the nations. He then spoke of how and why God would bring them back in a time of distress.

> *The Lord will scatter you among the peoples, and you will be left few in number among the nations where the Lord drives you. There you will serve gods, the work of man's hands, wood and stone, which neither see nor hear nor eat nor smell. But from there you will seek the Lord your God, and you will find Him if you search for Him with all your heart and all your soul. When you are in distress and all these things have come upon you, in the latter days you will return to the Lord your God and listen to His voice. For the Lord your God is a compassionate God; He will not fail you nor destroy you nor forget the covenant with your fathers which He swore to them.*
> **Deuteronomy 4:27-31**

He then used his last discourse in the book to speak directly to the last generation, even writing them a second song of deliverance (Deuteronomy 32). The other prophets add numerous details to the plan, and the New Testament summarizes and presents the entire end-time scenario like a drama filled with grandeur and mystery within the Book of Revelation.

**GOD HAS PLANNED FOR ANOTHER EXODUS**

THREE

# HOW DOES GOD SAVE ALL ISRAEL?

In the Book of Romans, the Apostle Paul lays out a powerful argument for justification by faith. It is not that he is taking issue with the Law of Moses or the teachings therein, he is establishing the law by focusing on the promises of God made to the fathers Abraham, Isaac, and Jacob.

> *Do we then nullify the Law through faith? May it never be! On the contrary, we establish the Law.* **Romans 3:31**

It is upon the promises made to the Fathers that Paul justifies his own ministry of reaching out to the nations. God promised the Fathers that their descendants would be as the stars of the night and as the sand of the sea. Not only would they be numerous, but they would come from all tribes, peoples, and tongues, and that in their *seed* would "all of the families of the earth be blessed" (Genesis 12:3). According to Paul, God preached the Gospel first to Abraham intending it to be preached to all peoples.

> *The Scripture, foreseeing that God would justify the Gentiles by faith, preached the gospel beforehand to Abraham, saying, "All the nations will be blessed in you."*
> **Galatians 3:8**

But there are natural questions that emerge from God's extensive promises. Does physical birth from the fathers automatically qualify one to be a recipient of these promises, and how do others not of physical birth inherit them as well? Paul answers those questions in Romans chapter nine explaining that not all of Israel are Israel (Romans 9:6). In other words, not all those physically born of Israel will be part of the heritage. He goes on to remind us that Abraham's firstborn Ishmael did not receive the promise. Instead, it was Isaac. The same can be said for Isaac's firstborn Esau. He did not receive the blessing. It was Jacob who received the promised blessings. Paul argues that the true descendants, the ones who receive the promised kingdom, are the children of promise (by faith). "Born of the flesh" guarantees nothing in God's plan.

> *That is, it is not the children of the flesh who are children of God, but the children of the promise are regarded as descendants.* **Romans 9:8**

It follows then that others, not physical descendants, who believe in the same God and are adopted into the family are the true heirs. He illustrates this promise by describing an olive tree (Israel) with natural and wild branches. All of the branches have been broken off and then must be grafted back into the tree. By the way, Jeremiah in his day defined Israel as "a green olive tree, beautiful in fruit and form." However, the faithless people of his days were referred to as "stripped away branches" (Jeremiah 5:10) and worthless "branches" (Jeremiah 11:16). Paul, built on the prophet's teaching to show the physical descendants of the fathers as natural branches that are grafted into the olive by faith in the promised Son (the Messiah) and the wild branches as those from the nations (all peoples, tribes, and tongues) who believe in the promises of God. Together, they are defined as the one olive tree Remnant Israel (the children of promise). Paul also offers a caution to the wild branches that have been grafted in.

## HOW DOES GOD SAVE ALL ISRAEL?

*But if some of the branches were broken off, and you, being a wild olive, were grafted in among them and became partaker with them of the rich root of the olive tree, do not be arrogant toward the branches; but if you are arrogant, remember that it is not you who supports the root, but the root supports you.* **Romans 11:17-18**

By the way, the term "Zion," aside from Israel, is a technical term used in the grafting of trees. Once a branch is spliced into the tree and bound tightly, after three days, if it is bonded, it is then called "Zion." The prophets of Israel used this term extensively to describe Israel and Jerusalem with the meaning of being "bonded" to the LORD.

Today, the Judeo-Christian world defines the inhabitants of the world as "Jews and Gentiles." In sharp contrast, the Scriptures define the world as believers and unbelievers of God. In fact, the term "Gentiles" is really a term for "unbelievers." Paul elaborates on the Scriptural definition of the world's inhabitants. He says that believers are **not** all physical descendants of Abraham; he says that some believers have been adopted into the family by faith. He also says that some physical descendants of Abraham are **not** heirs of Abraham at all. They have rejected the promises of God and want to be like the nations. Therefore, when Paul speaks of "all Israel," he is speaking of Remnant Israel defined by the Scriptures and **not** just the Jews of the world's definition.

It is using this Scriptural definition that Paul gives the most profound teaching of the *Greater Exodus* in the New Testament.

*For I do not want you, brethren, to be uninformed of this mystery—so that you will not be wise in your own estimation—that a partial hardening has happened to Israel until the fullness of the Gentiles has come in; and so all Israel will be saved; just as it is written, "The Deliverer will*

## HOW DOES GOD SAVE ALL ISRAEL?

*come from Zion, He will remove ungodliness from Jacob." "This is My covenant with them, when I take away their sins." From the standpoint of the gospel they are enemies for your sake, but from the standpoint of God's choice they are beloved for the sake of the fathers;...**Romans 11:25-28***

There is definitely a *mystery* of what Paul is talking about. Let me walk you through some of the questions that are asked. "What is 'the fullness of the Gentiles' and when is that completed?" "How can all of Israel be saved and does that really mean 'all' of them?" "The 'Deliverer' must be the Messiah, but what does it mean that He comes out of Zion?" "What covenant is God referring to when He says 'My covenant with them'," and "how does He 'take away their sins'?" Many Christians hold to the New Covenant for salvation, the Old Testament as history, and the path to God is through Jesus and the church. They don't believe God is going to revert to the past.

By the way, the biggest question in the passage above is what appears to be a direct quotation: *"The Deliverer will come from Zion, He will remove ungodliness from Jacob. This is My covenant with them, when I take away their sins."* Where is that verse in the Scriptures? Some teachers suggest Isaiah 59:20, which says *"A Redeemer will come TO Zion, and to those who turn from transgression in Jacob."* But let us examine the detailed phrases used in this passage before we determine the source of the quotation.

The *fullness of the Gentiles* is a Hebrew expression referring to Israel's exile to the nations. The House of Israel began their worldwide exile in 722-721 B.C. at the hand of the Assyrians. The House of Judah (commonly called the Jews) began their worldwide exile with the destruction of the temple in 70 A.D. and the Bar Kokhba revolution of 132-135 A.D. Since those days and to the present time we are in the age of the Gentiles.

## HOW DOES GOD SAVE ALL ISRAEL?

Some Jews have begun to return to the Land (the modern state of Israel); however, the worldwide exile of all Israel is still with us and we are in the age of the Gentiles until the remaining Israelites (both houses) return to the land.

The expression "all Israel" refers to Remnant Israel, and includes the two houses of Israel – the House of Ephraim (Israel) and the House of Judah. It also includes the "companions" of those two houses which are other people, tribes, and tongues of the nations who have joined with the remnant to follow the God of Israel.

The "Deliverer" is the Messiah whose throne is Jerusalem/Zion.

> *Now it will come about that in the last days the mountain of the house of the LORD will be established as the chief of the mountains, and will be raised above the hills; and all the nations will stream to it. And many peoples will come and say, "Come, let us go up to the mountain of the LORD, to the house of the God of Jacob; that He may teach us concerning His ways and that we may walk in His paths." For the law will go forth from Zion, and the word of the LORD from Jerusalem.* **Isaiah 2:2-3**

Many Jewish teachers consider this to be one of the most powerful prophecies of the Messiah, when He teaches Torah to the whole world. Paul's quotation is actually looking back at two psalms. These are unusual psalms because they are almost identical. Psalms 14 and 53 are identical with only a slight variation in a couple of the verses. The headers of these Psalms are entitled as "A Psalm of David" and "A Maskil of David." Both conclude with these words.

> *Oh, that the salvation of Israel would come out of Zion! When the LORD restores His captive people, Jacob will rejoice, Israel will be glad.* **Psalm 14:7**

21

## HOW DOES GOD SAVE ALL ISRAEL?

*Oh, that the salvation of Israel would come out of Zion! When God restores His captive people, let Jacob rejoice, let Israel be glad.* **Psalm 53:6**

This is what Paul is quoting from in Romans 11. So, what is being expressed here by David in the Psalms that Paul is so excited about? Psalms 14 and 53 first describe a great conflict that matches the description of the great tribulation, but it concludes with the cry for the Messiah to bring back the captives and the kingdom begins. This is exactly what the *Greater Exodus* is about! The key to the intent of the Psalms is the repetition. Any good Torah teacher will tell you that anytime Scripture repeats itself or appears to be redundant in expression, you should stop and take notice of something profound being said. This is the meaning of the title in the Psalm 53 "A Maskil of David." A Maskil is defined as a profound teaching with great insight.

Paul understood that something wonderful would take place at the end of the ages. He understood that God's goal was to deliver His people from the slavery of sin in the world. He understood that Messiah Yeshua was and is our Deliverer and our Salvation. Whatever was going to happen in the nations was simply the *"fullness of the Gentiles."* When that was complete, the *Greater Exodus* would bring God's people—His remnant—out of their slavery (out of the nations). Sin would be no more, just as David had said in his Psalms. Paul's understanding of God's plan was that of Isaiah as well.

*Listen to Me, you stubborn-minded, who are far from righteousness. I bring near My righteousness, it is not far off; and My salvation will not delay. And I will grant salvation in Zion, and My glory for Israel.* **Isaiah 46:12-13**

This passage in Romans 11:25-28 with "all Israel" being saved at the end has been confusing for many Christians. They have been led to believe in *replacement theology*. That is a theological scheme, which teaches that the work of redemption by the Messiah has rendered the Law of Moses null and void, that the blessings and future prophesies for Israel is now the property of the church, and the curses of the Law have fallen upon Israel, while all the blessings have been morphed into the church. This is the primary reason why the "*Greater Exodus*" has not been taught to Christians. It is a series of prophecies focused on bringing Israel back from the nations, but *replacement theology* teaches that God is done with Israel, which is expressly contrary to the teaching and prophecy of Scripture.

Many evangelical Christians are not aware that the Catholics and many Protestant denominations do not believe that the nation of Israel is a fulfillment of prophecy today. They also do not believe that the people of Israel have a biblical right to the land of Israel (even though God promised the land to them). Sadly, they have relegated the Old Testament to biblical history, having no more authority in our lives today, and that the Law is done away with. Evangelical Christians view these points differently but they still hold onto some of the trappings of replacement theology, such as "the Law is done away with."

However, the Apostle Paul constantly quoted the Law and prophets referencing the Egyptian exodus for spiritual instruction in his day. Based on his writings, Paul would surely dispute the conclusions of churchmen today.

> *For I do not want you to be unaware, brethren, that our fathers were all under the cloud and all passed through the sea; and all were baptized into Moses in the cloud and in the sea; and all ate the same spiritual food; and all drank the same spiritual drink, for they were drinking from a spiritual rock which followed them; and the rock was Messiah. Nevertheless, with most of them God was*

*not well-pleased; for they were laid low in the wilderness. Now these things happened as examples for us, so that we should not crave evil things as they also craved. Do not be idolaters, as some of them were; as it is written, "The people sat down to eat and drink, and stood up to play." Nor let us act immorally, as some of them did, and twenty-three thousand fell in one day. Nor let us try the Lord, as some of them did, and were destroyed by the serpents. Nor grumble, as some of them did, and were destroyed by the destroyer. Now these things happened to them as an example, and they were written for our instruction, upon whom the ends of the ages have come.* **1 Corinthians 10:1-11**

Paul saw a number of parallels of instruction for our faith in the Messiah from the exodus story. He saw the cloud and the crossing of the Red Sea like unto baptism. He compared the water from the Rock and the manna from heaven as drink and bread from the Messiah Himself. He saw the disobedience of the people in the wilderness as admonitions and lessons we should learn today. Then he concludes by announcing the story of the exodus is for our instruction—that this will happen at the end of the ages.

There is more to what Paul said in comparing the story of the Egyptian exodus to what is coming at the end of the ages. The fact is Paul was only summarizing an extensive subject in the Scriptures, ranging from Moses through the prophets. Moses didn't just recount the exodus from Egypt, he also spoke directly to the last generation describing the exodus they would have a part in. The prophets key off of Moses and lay out the Messiah's part in our final redemption at the end of the ages. Now that we see the New Testament, and the Apostle Paul references the Egyptian exodus as part of our instruction and future, let us examine the message of Moses much deeper, especially the message to "the generation to come."

FOUR

# HAVING EYES TO SEE AND EARS TO HEAR

Moses taught about the *Greater Exodus* in his final discourse in the Book of Deuteronomy. Typically, the systematic teaching of the Torah divides the first five books into weekly portions taught over a one year period. The exception is that some teachers follow a three year order. However you slice it, each Sabbath a particular portion is traditionally taught. The annual cycle has the Book of Deuteronomy being taught just before the fall holidays in August and September. The Torah portion beginning at Deuteronomy 29:10 is entitled "Nitzavim," which means "standing." Moses gathered all the people of Israel including the humblest in the camp—the man who gathers the firewood and woman who fetches the water. Moses wanted to speak to every person in the camp, including the native born and the aliens and sojourners who were traveling with them, because he had something extraordinary to say.

"I'm not talking to the people here today!" So, who was Moses talking to? He identified his target audience as "the generation to come" (Deuteronomy 29:22). Jewish sages say that Moses was speaking to the future last generation. This is the same future generation that Yeshua spoke of when He spoke of the end times saying that generation will not pass away until all is completed (Matthew 24:34).

Obviously, Moses wanted the people with him to hear the same message. He went on to explain that those with him would enter the land but not be faithful, and that in later generations God would cast them out of the land and into the nations.

> ...and the LORD uprooted them from their land in anger and in fury and in great wrath, and cast them into another land, as it is this day. **Deuteronomy 29:28**

This same message is given by Moses in greater detail in the Book of Leviticus.

> *$^{27}$Yet if in spite of this, you do not obey Me, but act with hostility against Me,... $^{33}$You, however, I will scatter among the nations and will draw out a sword after you, as your land becomes desolate and your cities become waste. $^{38}$But you will perish among the nations, and your enemies' land will consume you.* **Leviticus 26:27, 33, 38**

Moses didn't say God would reject Israel completely or replace them when the Messiah came. Instead, he explained that God would ultimately gather them again. They would be brought back from of all of the remote and different places they had been scattered to, and God would bring them back to the same promised land.

> *Yet in spite of this, when they are in the land of their enemies, I will not reject them, nor will I so abhor them as to destroy them, breaking My covenant with them; for I am the LORD their God. But I will remember for them the covenant with their ancestors, whom I brought out of the land of Egypt in the sight of the nations, that I might be their God. I am the LORD.* **Leviticus 26:44-45**

You should note that God has purposed to bring Israel back from the nations based on the purposes and the covenant that were established at the Egyptian exodus. Moses said that the final generation would know of Israel's history (the blessings and the curses) and would eventually turn back to the Lord and return to the teaching of His commandments.

> *So it shall be when all of these things have come upon you, the blessing and the curse which I have set before you, and you call them to mind in all nations where the Lord your God has banished you, and you return to the Lord your God and obey Him with all your heart and soul according to all that I command you today, you and your sons, then the Lord your God will restore you from captivity, and have compassion on you, and will gather you again from all the peoples where the Lord your God has scattered you. If your outcasts are at the ends of the earth, from there the Lord your God will gather you, and from there He will bring you back. The Lord your God will bring you into the land which your fathers possessed, and you shall possess it; and He will prosper you and multiply you more than your fathers. Moreover the Lord your God will circumcise your heart and the heart of your descendants, to love the Lord your God with all your heart and with all your soul, so that you may live. The Lord your God will inflict all these curses on your enemies and on those who hate you, who persecuted you. And you shall again obey the Lord, and observe all His commandments which I command you today. Then the Lord your God will prosper you abundantly in all the work of your hand, in the offspring of your body and in the offspring of your cattle and in the produce of your ground, for the Lord will again rejoice over you for good, just as He rejoiced over your fathers; if you obey the Lord your God to keep His commandments and His statutes which are written in this book of the law, if you turn to the Lord your God with all your heart and soul.* **Deuteronomy 30:1-10**

Remembering that Moses is speaking to the final generation, what has he just declared? Moses makes a strong case to return to the Torah and keep the greatest commandment of the Law "with all their hearts." He stated that returning to the Torah would be an important part of God's gathering them from the "ends of the earth." This is fundamental because some of the commandments are directly related to the preparation needed for the *Greater Exodus*, such as keeping the feasts of Passover and Tabernacles. Passover is crucial to understanding when the *Greater Exodus* begins and the Feast of Tabernacles physically prepares you and your family for the journey! Moses says that God is going to bring them back to the very land promised to Abraham and his descendants (the Remnant). When I view a map of the Middle East, I can see the journey from Egypt to Israel. Yet when I look at a globe of the earth, my eyes cannot see the entire journey for the *Greater Exodus*. Moses says it will happen "from the ends of the earth."

Obeying the basic commandments in the Torah sustained the mixed multitude (native Israel and aliens) in the wilderness so that they could be civil and appropriate with one another, even in a mobile camping environment. These same commandments will be essential to Remnant Israel escaping in the *Greater Exodus* and organizing themselves. Anything less will be mob rule and a human disaster.

Turning again to Moses' discourse in "Nitzavim," we see him explain a dramatic difference between the generation he was standing with and the generation he was talking to. This difference is critical to understanding the prophecies of the *Greater Exodus* and applying the lessons learned from the exodus.

> *And Moses summoned all Israel and said to them, "You have seen all that the* L<small>ORD</small> *did before your eyes in the land of Egypt to Pharaoh and all his servants and all his land;*

*the great trials which your eyes have seen, those great signs and wonders. Yet to this day the LORD has not given you a heart to know, nor eyes to see, nor ears to hear. I have led you forty years in the wilderness; your clothes have not worn out on you, and your sandal has not worn out on your foot."* **Deuteronomy 29:2-5**

Despite the children of Israel seeing the judgments of God on the Egyptians, crossing the Red Sea, hearing the voice of God at Mount Sinai, constructing the tabernacle in the wilderness, and following the cloud by day and fire by night – despite all of this – Moses said that God had not yet given them eyes to see, ears to hear, nor a heart of understanding. What is it that they couldn't see or hear?

Isaiah referred to this same matter in his day, repeating Moses' complaint of not remembering or learning the lessons of the past.

*Oh, that You would rend the heavens and come down, that the mountains might quake at Your presence—as fire kindles the brushwood, as fire causes water to boil—to make Your name known to Your adversaries, that the nations may tremble at Your presence! When You did awesome things which we did not expect, You came down, the mountains quaked at Your presence. For from days of old they have not heard nor perceived by ear, nor has the eye seen a God besides You, Who acts in behalf of the one who waits for Him.* **Isaiah 64:1-4**

Isaiah referenced how God came down on the mountain and spoke His commandments to Israel. Yet, Isaiah said in his day that Israel still didn't hear or see what God is doing. They still don't get it!

The Apostle Paul echoed both Moses and Isaiah on this point, but then he announced that we can see and hear what God wants us to know. Paul argues that the Messiah has given us the gift of the Holy Spirit which enables us to see, hear, and understand God's purposes and plans for us.

> *But just as it is written, "Things which eye has not seen and ear has not heard, and which have not entered the heart of man, all that God has prepared for those who love Him." For to us God revealed them through the Spirit; for the Spirit searches all things, even the depths of God.*
> **1 Corinthians 2:9-10**

Paul taught us that we are to see, hear, and understand future things not understood by the generation that left Egypt or was scattered out of Israel. He goes on to say that God's wisdom is now available to us, that our faith is not based on the wisdom of men, but on the power of God. If we are to see and hear the message of the *Greater Exodus*, then it must be with the aid of the Holy Spirit.

Here is some good news that goes with this end-time teaching. God will pour out His Spirit on us so that we can see, hear, and understand the *Greater Exodus*. Ezekiel speaks of when the exile to the nations will end, and God will pour out His Spirit on the whole house of Israel (Ezekiel 39:29), and the prophet Joel says that God's Spirit will be poured out and everyone will speak of the prophecy (Joel 2:28).

Moses said that the children of Israel leaving Egypt couldn't see, hear, or understand God's purpose. Isaiah said the same for his generation. They didn't understand because the Holy Spirit had not been given yet. So what about today? How are we to understand this prophecy and teaching prior to the great outpouring? It still has to come by way of the Spirit.

I believe that many of us can understand this teaching by the Holy Spirit just as Moses and Paul did. However, we need to be committed to following the "instructions in righteousness" and believing what Moses wrote first. If we diminish or dismiss the teaching of Moses, there is no path to understanding. Isaiah asserts it this way:

> *To the law and to the testimony! If they do not speak according to this word, it is because they have no dawn.*
> **Isaiah 8:20**

"Having no dawn" means that you have no light of understanding, just like the expression "It just dawned on me!" Yeshua spoke to this same point with regard to His own teaching.

> *But if you do not believe his* [Moses] *writings, how will you believe My words?* **John 5:47**

Now turning back to Moses, what else did he say in "Nitzavim?"

The message from Moses given in Deuteronomy 30:1-10 is followed by a strong exhortation on how to actually take and receive the promised land. Not only were his words appropriate to those standing there, but they are even more profound for the final generation.

> *The Lord is the one who goes ahead of you; He will be with you. He will not fail you or forsake you. Do not fear or be dismayed.* **Deuteronomy 31:8**

This is followed by a second song of deliverance in Deuteronomy 32. Truly, Moses wasn't giving this song to those standing there that day. He was speaking to the final generation urging them to prepare for an even *Greater Exodus*, one based on the exodus out of Egypt. But to understand this, you must have eyes to see and ears to hear. The Book of Revelation confirms this when it says that the tribulation saints will sing two songs.

> *And they sang the song of Moses, the bond-servant of God, and the song of the Lamb, saying, Great and marvelous are Your works, O Lord God, the Almighty; righteous and true are Your ways, King of the nations!* **Revelation 15:3**

Moses is not the only prophet with the message and prophecy of the *Greater Exodus*. Look at how Isaiah paints the picture of the future exodus.

> *"I will set a sign among them and will send survivors from them to the nations: Tarshish, Put, Lud, Meshech, Tubal, and Javan, to the distant coastlands that have neither heard My fame nor seen My glory. And they will declare My glory among the nations. Then they shall bring all your brethren from all the nations as a grain offering to the Lord, on horses, in chariots, in litters, on mules, and on camels, to My holy mountain Jerusalem," says the Lord, "just as the sons of Israel bring their grain offering in a clean vessel to the house of the Lord." "I will also take some of them for priests and for Levites," says the Lord. "For just as the new heavens and the new earth which I make will endure before Me," declares the Lord, "So your offspring and your name will endure."* **Isaiah 66:19-22**

Bringing your brethren from the nations as a grain offering is the picture of many brethren coming to the Lord; journeying by different modes to Jerusalem sounds like an exodus out of many nations. This is correct; he is describing an exodus journey.

Anyone can have knowledge of the *Greater Exodus* just reading Scripture; however, the understanding of the prophecies is revealed by the Spirit of God. I believe this is the reason why the teaching and the understanding of the *Greater Exodus* is not wide-spread. God reveals it to His people based on their faith and obedience to the Holy Spirit.

Ironically, Judaism does not believe in Messiah Yeshua, yet seems to understand that there will be a *Greater Exodus* in the future, while Christianity does believe in the Messiah but doesn't seem to have a clue about the future exodus. I can understand how Christians are in this dilemma. *Replacement theology*, which focuses primarily on the New Covenant, has diminished the "Old Covenant" and reduced the exodus story to history. It is tragic since the exodus story is the base teaching in Scripture for redemption, salvation, deliverance, and the future kingdom. The blood of the Lamb in the exodus story is the same for us in the New Covenant with a personal testimony of redemption (being purchased out of slavery to sin). Failing to understand this leads to shallowness in the faith today. It then follows that not appreciating the exodus diminishes the ability to see a future *Greater Exodus*. Christians could learn much about their faith in the Messiah and their future if they could see what Jews see and believe about the future exodus. Let me show you.

FIVE

# WHY JUDAISM BELIEVES IN THE GREATER EXODUS

If you have attempted to share your belief in Yeshua of Nazareth as the Messiah with a religious Jew, you may have been surprised to hear them reject your effort due to the fact that Yeshua did **not** fulfill all of the Messianic prophecies. When evangelical Christians hear this they are generally mystified. They have a tendency to think that "all that stuff in the Old Testament" was fulfilled somehow when Yeshua came the first time. They have no idea what the Jewish person is talking about or the prophecies that he is referencing. But Jews know that there are great prophecies of the future—when the Messiah leads back the scattered exiles of Israel! This did not happen when Yeshua of Nazareth was here, so they conclude that He is not the Messiah.

Yeshua of Nazareth is the Messiah and He did accomplish the prophecies of the *redemption*, but the prophecies of the *restoration* are at the end of the ages. Therefore, the Messiah will yet accomplish them just as He said He would. Judaism doesn't understand that the work of redemption (the blood of the Lamb) is separate from the future restoration. Restoration is still a future element as part of the end-time events including the *day of the* Lord and the Resurrection. Many Christian brethren believe in the redemption but virtually ignore the future restoration. Yet the prophets of Israel state that the Messiah does both, first as a suffering servant, then as a returning King.

Judaism failed to understand that the exile to the nations was not complete when Yeshua first came. The House of Judah was not yet scattered worldwide. It followed the destruction of Jerusalem in 70 A.D. Therefore, Yeshua could not fulfill the prophecies of gathering both houses from worldwide exile and bring them (Israel and Judah) together until the "fullness of the Gentiles" was complete. The "fullness of the Gentiles" is another pattern from the exodus. God did not bring the children of Israel out of Egypt until the iniquity of the Amorites was complete. This is exactly what God prophesied to Abram.

> *Then in the fourth generation they will return here, for the iniquity of the Amorite is not yet complete.* **Genesis 15:16**

Why did God mention anything about the Amorites in the timing of bringing Israel out of Egypt? It is because God used the children of Israel coming out of Egypt to judge King Sihon and the Amorites. This particular battle increased Israel's combat strength and their reputation in taking the land. In the same way, God has said that the *Greater Exodus* will not happen until the "fullness of the Gentiles." God intends to judge the whole world when He brings His people out of the nations!

In the days of Yeshua, the House of Judah had returned from Babylonian captivity, which occurred as a judgment upon Judah for failing to keep the Sabbatical year (giving the land rest every seven years). When they had been in the land 490 years and had failed to keep the Schmitah (Sabbath rest for the land) seventy times, they were sent to Babylon for the seventy years (Jeremiah 29:10). This is confirmed in the book of 2 Chronicles.

## WHY JUDAISM BELIEVES IN THE GREATER EXODUS

> *Those who had escaped from the sword he carried away to Babylon; and they were servants to him and to his sons until the rule of the kingdom of Persia, to fulfill the word of the LORD by the mouth of Jeremiah, until the land had enjoyed its sabbaths. All the days of its desolation it kept sabbath until seventy years were complete.*
> ***2 Chronicles 36:20-21***

Yeshua came after the Babylonian exile/return and before the worldwide exile. He was there to fulfill the "Lamb of God" prophecies and to make a way for us to receive personal redemption. The stage would then be set to share the good news that the Messiah would then take us to the kingdom. The same pattern came from the exodus. Being redeemed out of Egypt was the work of the Lamb, but the trip to the "promised land" (the kingdom) is something else. Yeshua has fulfilled the redemption part, we are still looking for the restoration and His leading of the *Greater Exodus*.

When the prophets of Israel prophesy about the Messiah, it is generally in the context of Him being a part of the *Greater Exodus*. Many Bible teachers refer to the message of the Messiah as the Gospel (the Good News), and they are right, but what they fail to understand in the Gospel is the message of the *Greater Exodus* coming to the scattered exiles! Just as Moses was raised up to lead the people out of Egypt, so the Messiah is prophesied to be raised up from His countrymen to lead His people to the "promised land." Let's examine some of these prophecies to see why the Jews place so much emphasis on the Messiah gathering the scattered exiles (the Good News).

> *I will raise up a prophet from among their countrymen like you, and I will put My words in his mouth, and he shall speak to them all that I command him. It shall come about*

*that whoever will not listen to My words which he shall speak in My name, I Myself will require it of him.*
**Deuteronomy 18:18-19**

This is a dramatic prophecy of the Messiah to come; it is the one from God to Moses. Why is the *prophet* (the Messiah) to be like Moses? Jewish Answer: He leads another exodus. This then is the basis for the prophets to speak of the future Messiah. He is to have even more prestige than Moses had, and He will deliver and save the captives of Israel. Here is a powerful example from Isaiah where the Messiah describes Himself in the language of the *Greater Exodus*.

*Listen to Me, O islands, and pay attention, you peoples from afar. The* L ORD *called Me from the womb; from the body of My mother He named Me. He has made My mouth like a sharp sword, in the shadow of His hand He has concealed Me; and He has also made Me a select arrow, He has hidden Me in His quiver. He said to Me, "You are My Servant, Israel, in Whom I will show My glory." But I said, "I have toiled in vain, I have spent My strength for nothing and vanity; yet surely the justice due to Me is with the* L ORD*, and My reward with My God."* **Isaiah 49:1-4**

This is a specific prophecy about the Messiah, but the proclamation of the message is to the *islands* and those *far away*. This is the common language in Scripture for those scattered away from the land of Israel. This is not a message that the Hebrew Messiah would leave Israel and then become the "Christ" of the nations. The context and remainder of this passage is about the Messiah and the people of Israel. The Messiah was physically conceived in the *womb* of Mary. He was *named* while in the womb by the Angel Gabriel (Matthew 1:20-21). The Messiah is the One whose mouth has a *sharp sword* and is a *select arrow hidden in the Father's quiver* (Isaiah 49:2). He is also the *Ser-*

*vant* of the LORD who shows the *glory* of His Father (verse 3). These are definitions of the Messiah to come (the Moses of the future exodus). But then the last phrase is about Israel scattered, *yet surely the justice due to Me is with the LORD, and My reward with My God* (verse 4). The *justice due* is the cry of desperation and great concern on the part of those scattered. The concern is for those who think that God has forsaken them. To be convinced of this conclusion, one only needs to review the history of Israel and the Jewish people scattered these last 2,000 years suffering under the pogroms (organized massacres or persecutions of minorities), expulsions, ghettos, and the holocaust.

The oldest known Jewish sermon in the Bible is found in the Book of Isaiah. Using the prophecies of the Messiah-to-come and His part in the *Greater Exodus*, there is an ancient homiletic teaching called "The Haftorahs of Consolation." A *homiletic* teaching in this instance is where the rabbis have taken numerous Scriptures from the Book of Isaiah to create a teaching on the subject of *the Consolation of Israel*. This particular homiletic teaching dates prior to the Messiah. Religious Jews have heard this sermon every year during the final seven Sabbaths leading to the Feast of Trumpets. It begins in Isaiah chapter 40 and extends to the latter chapters. *Haftorahs* are parallel teachings written by the prophets that are taught along with the weekly Torah teachings. The Haftorahs of Consolation tell the story of scattered Israel crying out from the nations, fearing that they have been forsaken by God. The homiletic message is really a message of hope, offering consolation by remembering God's promise to gather them again and bring them back to the promised land. The specific words of Isaiah that summarize the sermon are "the consolation of Israel, the redemption of Jerusalem." It is part of the conclusion of the Torah teaching and preparation for the fall holidays of Trumpets, Atonement, and Tabernacles. These holidays prophetically speak of the end of the ages, the future resurrection, the *day of the LORD*, and the Messiah's return to establish His Kingdom.

The historical teaching of this sermon is evidenced in the New Testament. The Gospel of Luke tells of two people who were taught this sermon and how Mary and Joseph encountered them when they brought Yeshua to the temple for the first time. The first person they met was a man named Simeon. See what Simeon had been taught and believed.

> *And there was a man in Jerusalem whose name was Simeon; and this man was righteous and devout, looking for the consolation of Israel; and the Holy Spirit was upon him. And it had been revealed to him by the Holy Spirit that he would not see death before he had seen the Lord's Messiah.*
> **Luke 2:25-26**

Looking for the "consolation of Israel" is the ancient sermon of the Haftorahs of Consolation today. The Jewish expectation of the Messiah in that day was that He would gather those scattered abroad (exiles from the House of Israel) in far-away places (remotest parts of the earth) and bring them back to the promised land. There was a second person they met in the temple that day.

> *And there was a prophetess, Anna the daughter of Phanuel, of the tribe of Asher. She was advanced in years and had lived with her husband seven years after her marriage, and then as a widow to the age of eighty-four. She never left the temple, serving night and day with fastings and prayers. At that very moment she came up and began giving thanks to God, and continued to speak of Him to all those who were looking for the redemption of Jerusalem.*
> **Luke 2:36-38**

The expression the "redemption of Jerusalem" shows that Anna and Simeon were looking for one particular Messiah. They testified of their expectations while Yeshua was a baby

## WHY JUDAISM BELIEVES IN THE GREATER EXODUS

that He was the one they were looking for. Here is how Isaiah presents this ancient sermon.

> *How lovely on the mountains are the feet of him who brings good news, who announces peace and brings good news of happiness, who announces salvation, and says to Zion, "Your God reigns!" Listen! Your watchmen lift up their voices, they shout joyfully together; for they will see with their own eyes when the LORD restores Zion. Break forth, shout joyfully together, you waste places of Jerusalem; for the LORD has comforted His people, He has redeemed Jerusalem. The LORD has bared His holy arm in the sight of all the nations, that all the ends of the earth may see the* **salvation** *of our God.* **Isaiah 52:7-10**

Simeon believed Isaiah's prophecy and was looking for the Messiah. Here is his declaration:

> *Now Lord, You are releasing your bond-servant to depart in peace, according to Your word; for my eyes have seen Your* **salvation, Luke 2:29-30**

By the way, the Hebrew word for **salvation** is "Yeshua," the name of the Messiah.

Just as Simeon and Anna held to this prophecy, so too do religious Jews today. They are looking for the consolation and redemption of another exodus, an exodus that is to be led by the Messiah (the One greater than Moses). The very next verses of Isaiah's passage briefly define the future *Greater Exodus* which the Messiah leads.

> *Depart, depart, go out from there, touch nothing unclean; go out of the midst of her, purify yourselves, you who carry the vessels of the LORD. But you will not go out in haste,*

> *nor will you go as fugitives; for the Lord will go before you, and the God of Israel will be your rear guard.*
> **Isaiah 52:11-12**

In the exodus from Egypt, the children of Israel cried out for God's deliverance. God responded to this cry in accordance to His plan given to Abraham by enlisting Moses. God's plan required four generations and at least 400 years after the prophecy was given. Remember, God wanted the iniquity of the Amorites to be full as well. Did that mean that He was ignoring the plight of His people in Egyptian bondage? Of course not.

> *The Lord said, "I have surely seen the affliction of My people who are in Egypt, and have given heed to their cry because of their taskmasters, for I am aware of their sufferings."* **Exodus 3:7**

In the future exodus there will be another cry—a cry of being forsaken by God because of the exile to the nations. The world will become a very dangerous place for His people. This has been the consistent pattern for God's people. The Jewish people, in particular, have cried out like this throughout history. As the "time of distress" comes upon the whole world, all believers will eventually cry out as the Jewish people have. And just as God heard them earlier in Egypt, so He will hear those from the nations in the future. This is the meaning of why Isaiah speaks of God consoling as well as redeeming. Here is how the cry of the future will sound as given in the homiletic teaching and God's response to the cry.

> *But Zion said, "The Lord has forsaken me, and the Lord has forgotten me." Can a woman forget her nursing child, and have no compassion on the son of her womb? Even these may forget, but I will not forget you.*
> **Isaiah 49:14-15**

## WHY JUDAISM BELIEVES IN THE GREATER EXODUS

Some of those scattered will consider their situation too difficult for an escape and a *Greater Exodus*. The Lord through Isaiah offers this consolation message to them.

> *"Can the prey be taken from the mighty man, or the captives of a tyrant be rescued?" Surely, thus says the Lord, "Even the captives of the mighty man will be taken away, and the prey of the tyrant will be rescued; for I will contend with the one who contends with you, and I will save your sons. I will feed your oppressors with their own flesh, and they will become drunk with their own blood as with sweet wine; and all flesh will know that I, the Lord, am your Savior, and your Redeemer, the Mighty One of Jacob."*
> **Isaiah 49:24-26**

There are some Christian denominations who argue that the prophecies of a *future Israel* have been rendered null and void because of Israel's rejection of the Messiah. Some Dispensationalists allow for a *future Israel*, but they disconnect themselves from it. Yet the prophecies even have an answer for that argument.

> *Thus says the Lord, "Where is the certificate of divorce, by which I have sent your mother away? Or to whom of My creditors did I sell you? Behold, you were sold for your iniquities, and for your transgressions your mother was sent away. Why was there no man when I came? When I called, why was there none to answer? Is My hand so short that it cannot ransom? Or have I no power to deliver? Behold, I dry up the sea with My rebuke, I make the rivers a wilderness; their fish stink for lack of water and die of thirst. I clothe the heavens with blackness, and I make sackcloth their covering."* **Isaiah 50:1-3**

For those who think that the "church" is something different from Israel, consider this. The word "church" is translated from the Greek word "ecclesia," which means the "called out assembly." The first use of this Greek word in the Greek Septuagint (the Old Testament Scriptures translated into Greek) refers to the "called out assembly" from Egypt. The children of Israel were the first "church." The only reason why you don't read it that way today is because Bible translators use the word "assembly" for Israel and "church" for Christians. They wanted them to be separate and distinct, but God does not see it that way. What God started with the fathers has continued and will continue all the way to the Messiah's return and His kingdom, the same kingdom promised to Abraham.

The LORD can deliver anyone He chooses. By His own word, He has sworn to deliver all those who believe in the God of Israel. It should not shock you then to understand that the New Testament quotes from these portions of Isaiah more than it quotes from any other passage in the Scriptures when explaining that the Messiah is our Savior. These are all of the prophecies of Isaiah, the teaching we call today "the consolation of Israel and the redemption of Jerusalem!"

Simeon and Anna were devout Jews in the days of Yeshua. When Yeshua came as a baby, they instantly recognized Him because they had been taught to expect a Messiah savior. They had been instructed that while God had judged Israel and punished her, the God of Israel would not go so far as to completely reject Israel. Instead, they were convinced that God would raise up another like Moses who would lead them back. They believed that the Messiah would comfort them and would redeem them. They believed in this future Messiah and that He would lead the future exodus. They were correct to believe this.

Present day Judaism is looking for the "consolation of Israel and the redemption of Jerusalem" just as Simeon and Anna did. They pray daily the Tefilat HaAmidah, "The Standing Prayer," also called the *Shemoneh Esrei* (Shemoneh Esrei "The Eighteen," in reference to the original number of constituent blessings; there are now nineteen), is the central prayer of Jewish liturgy. The tenth blessing is called *Kibbutz Galuyot* when they pray for the scattered exiles and petition God to bring them back. Jews pray daily for the *Greater Exodus*.

*Sound the great shofar for our freedom and raise a banner to gather our exiles and unite us together from the four corners of the earth. Blessed are You, L*ord*, who regathers the scattered of His people Israel.*

SIX

# ENDING THE EXILE AND WORKING TOWARD RESTORATION

God's punishment of the Whole House of Israel's exile to the nations must end before there can be a *Greater Exodus*. God's plan requires some very specific elements to be completed, but fundamental to any definition of a *return* is the fact that God's judgment of being exiled must be completed. Until God says that judgment is complete, there cannot be a return.

Ezekiel has prophesied that there is a day coming when God will declare the end of the exile to the nations. Yet He also wants everyone to know why Israel went into exile to begin with. God remembers and wants us to remember. People who don't remember are doomed to repeat past mistakes. This mistake of failing to remember has been made repeatedly, but we dare not make that mistake at the end of the ages.

> *"The nations will know that the house of Israel went into exile for their iniquity because they acted treacherously against Me, and I hid My face from them; so I gave them into the hand of their adversaries, and all of them fell by the sword. According to their uncleanness and according to their transgressions I dealt with them, and I hid My face from them."* **Ezekiel 39:23-24**

## ENDING THE EXILE AND WORKING TOWARD RESTORATION

The declaration to end the exile is the first step toward the *Greater Exodus*. Those who are part of the *Greater Exodus* must put all the past mistakes (those made by Israel in the past) behind them. God is going to end the cycle of Israel's not remembering His promises and purposes and repeated mistakes. Somehow, God is going to help us to forget the ways of the past.

> *Therefore thus says the Lord GOD, "Now I shall restore the fortunes of Jacob, and have mercy on the whole house of Israel; and I will be jealous for My holy name. They will forget their disgrace and all their treachery which they perpetrated against Me, when they live securely on their own land with no one to make them afraid. When I bring them back from the peoples and gather them from the lands of their enemies, then I shall be sanctified through them in the sight of the many nations."* **Ezekiel 39:25-27**

With the exception of a remnant, Israel rejected Yeshua as the Messiah. They abhorred Him, but this did not cause the God of Israel to forsake Israel. Instead, God judged them and sent them into the nations separated from His compassion and blessings of the land, while His future promises remained intact.

Isaiah also describes the rejection of Yeshua as the Messiah, with the future promise to keep the remnant intact (the LORD will never completely reject His people). God has promised to bring the Messiah forth to preserve the tribes of Israel.

> *And now says the LORD, who formed Me from the womb to be His Servant, to bring Jacob back to Him, so that Israel might be gathered to Him (for I am honored in the sight of the LORD, and My God is My strength), He says, "It is too small a thing that You should be My Servant to raise up the tribes of Jacob and to restore the preserved ones of Israel; I will also make You a light of the nations so that*

> *My salvation may reach to the end of the earth." Thus says the* LORD, *the Redeemer of Israel, and its Holy One, to the despised One, to the One abhorred by the nation, to the Servant of rulers, "Kings will see and arise, princes will also bow down; because of the* LORD *who is faithful, the Holy One of Israel who has chosen You."* **Isaiah 49:5-7**

This is a fascinating passage in just trying to understand who is speaking. At first, we hear the Messiah speaking of Himself being formed in a womb and His task to bring back Jacob. Then the voice shifts to the Father, who has anointed the Messiah, but then the final statement from the LORD seems to come from the Spirit when He says *"the Holy One of Israel who has chosen You."* For those who are perplexed by the plurality of God, this is definitely a troubling text. However, for us the anointing of the Messiah is purposed for our return, spiritually and physically. Israel is to be gathered to the Messiah. God is to be honored by this. All of the tribes of Jacob will be affected and the nations will hear the message to the ends of the earth. This same Messiah will be called the *Redeemer of Israel*, the *Holy One*, the *Despised One*, the *One abhorred by the nations*, the *Servant*, and the *Holy One of Israel*. It has always been a mystery to religious Jews as to how their Messiah could be called the *Redeemer of Israel* and the *One abhorred by the nations*. The mystery is solved in the Messiahship of Yeshua of Nazareth and His rejection by His own brethren.

This passage specifically says that the Messiah *My Servant* will raise up the tribes of Jacob. This is specific and goes back to the original definition for Israel. The present day definition of Israel is the "Jews." The *Greater Exodus* includes Jews, the other tribes of Israel making up the Northern Kingdom (the House of Israel), and many Gentiles—any of those in the nations who want to seek the God of Israel. Consider this passage describing the *Greater Exodus* and the location of those gathered.

## ENDING THE EXILE AND WORKING TOWARD RESTORATION

> *Thus says the L*ORD*, "In a favorable time I have answered You, and in a day of salvation I have helped You; and I will keep You and give You for a covenant of the people, to restore the land, to make them inherit the desolate heritages; saying to those who are bound, 'Go forth,' to those who are in darkness, 'Show yourselves.' Along the roads they will feed, and their pasture will be on all bare heights. They will not hunger or thirst, nor will the scorching heat or sun strike them down; for He who has compassion on them will lead them, and will guide them to springs of water. I will make all My mountains a road, and My highways will be raised up. Behold, these shall come from afar; and lo, these will come from the north and from the west, and these from the land of Sinim". Shout for joy, O heavens! And rejoice, O earth! Break forth into joyful shouting, O mountains! For the L*ORD *has comforted His people, and will have compassion on His afflicted.* **Isaiah 49:8-13**

The Messiah has been given to us as a covenant (the New Covenant) to be our salvation and for our gathering to the kingdom. The Messiah has promised to bring out the exiles of Israel from the nations, to show compassion to them, to comfort them, and to journey with them from the remotest parts of the earth, from the north and from the west, and from the land of *Sinim*. This is the message and joy of the Gospel! By the way, where exactly is the "land of Sinim" that He mentions? Answer: the areas and lands east of Israel. Today we refer to it as the Far East, including China and the Orient. It appears that this location was specifically cited to convey how extensive the *Greater Exodus* would be. Interestingly, many Christians in China and the Orient are awaiting the Messiah to return while suffering great persecution for their faith. The Messiah will bring the remnant back from every direction of the compass.

There is considerable evidence that Yeshua of Nazareth was teaching and doing things directly connected to the prophecies of the future *Greater Exodus*. In so doing, He was showing us that He was aware of those prophecies and did not ignore them, even though they were yet future. Consider these basic teachings we receive as Christians with almost hidden meanings to the *Greater Exodus*.

Yeshua is first introduced to Israel as the "Lamb of God" by John the Baptist. John was the prophesied forerunner of the Messiah preaching the "baptism of repentance." Scripture says that he was baptizing *in the wilderness* at the Jordan River when Yeshua came to him. It wasn't just ANY place at the Jordan River; it was the very place the children of Israel left the wilderness, crossed the Jordan, and entered the promised land led by Joshua. Many believers never heard that part in the teaching. The location is called "Qasr Al Yahud" (the crossing of the Jews) today. John's message and Yeshua's public ministry began exactly where ancient Israel completed the Egyptian exodus and entered the land of Israel. This is direct prophetic evidence that signifies that Yeshua and His message is an extension of the redemption from Egypt and God's original purposes. At this very crossing point, the LORD made the river Jordan dry just like at the crossing of the Red Sea, where Israel crossed into the promised land camping on the other side at Gilgal facing Jericho. This is the place where Joshua met the "Captain of the LORD's Host," which is one of the most pointed references to the Messiah leading them into the land. The Captain of the LORD's Host led Joshua and Israel to take and secure the promised land.

> *Now it came about when Joshua was by Jericho, that he lifted up his eyes and looked, and behold, a man was standing opposite him with his sword drawn in his hand, and Joshua went to him and said to him, "Are you for us or for our adversaries?" He said, "No; rather I indeed come now as captain of the host of the LORD." And Joshua fell*

> *on his face to the earth, and bowed down, and said to him, What has my lord to say to his servant?"* **Joshua 5:13-15**

Isn't it fascinating that Yeshua's first appearance as Messiah is in the same manner as the Captain of the LORD's Host appeared? Do you remember Yeshua's answer as to why He should be baptized there by John when John said that it was he who should be baptized by Him?

> *Then Yeshua arrived from Galilee at the Jordan coming to John, to be baptized by him. But John tried to prevent Him, saying, "I have need to be baptized by You, and do You come to me?" But Yeshua answering said to him, "Permit it at this time; for in this way it is fitting for us to fulfill all righteousness." Then he permitted Him.*
> **Matthew 3:13-15**

*Fulfilling all righteousness* was Yeshua's way of saying there was purpose in His coming to that place. Yeshua wasn't responding to John's message of repentance and then asking to be baptized. Yeshua didn't need His sins washed away! He wasn't repenting!

Most of us know about *baptism* (also *immersion*). We have been taught that it is something we do after receiving the LORD for salvation. It is a religious ritual that illustrates our sins being washed away; about the death, burial, and resurrection of the LORD; and is a public proclamation of our faith. However, there is much more to the Hebrew understanding of a mikveh (Hebrew for immersion).

At Mount Sinai, the LORD instructed Moses to have the people take a bath as preparation to hear the LORD speak on Mount Sinai (Exodus 19:10). The waters they immersed themselves in were the "living waters" from the Rock. "Living waters" are moving, natural waters as opposed to waters trapped in a container. The first people who were ever baptized (mikveh) were the children of Israel during the exodus. The Apostle Paul understood the greater significance of "baptism" and its part in the exodus. Listen to how he explains the cloud that led them and the Red Sea they crossed.

> *For I do not want you to be unaware, brethren, that our fathers were all under the cloud, and all passed through the sea; and all were baptized into Moses in the cloud and in the sea;* **1 Corinthians 10:1-2**

Baptism is part of the picture of leaving Egypt and the house of slavery behind. It is about transitioning from being a slave to being a free man. It is about being raised up as a "new man" who is redeemed by God.

So, what was the *righteousness* that Yeshua was *fulfilling* at His baptism? He chose the very place where the exodus ended (crossing the Jordan) to begin His ministry to all of Israel. The Messiah is not a *new* redemption, as perceived by most Christians; He is the original redemption (the Lamb of God) who leads us to the promised land. *Fulfilling righteousness* to the Messiah meant fulfilling all of the purposes of God, to bring all of Israel to His promised kingdom. Did not John say, "Repent, for the kingdom of God is at hand?"

What were the initial disciples expecting the Messiah to do? Answer: to lead back the scattered exiles in another *Greater Exodus*. Baptism is the ritual that reminded them of the cloud and the crossing of the sea. It was the preparation to hear the voice of God at the Mountain. They were looking for the "prophet like Moses." They were looking for the King and His kingdom to be established. They were looking for a Messiah Who would lead another exodus – a *Greater Exodus*.

Let me say it again, the Messiah's work of redemption is not different from the redemption from Egypt. His word was an extension of the same Passover story with the Lamb ("the Lamb of God"). Yeshua didn't start something new with His baptism. It was righteousness to be fulfilled; He was fulfilling God's purposes. It follows then that the story of the exodus was not to be shelved as mere history because the Messiah had come. It was the prophetic picture of the Messiah's work of redemption. Just as Moses lifted up his staff in the wilderness, so must the Son of Man be lifted up. Yeshua used the memorial Passover seder to commemorate the New Covenant which was compared with the covenant established in the exodus.

*"Behold, days are coming," declares the LORD, "when I will make a new covenant with the house of Israel and with the house of Judah, not like the covenant which I made with their fathers in the day I took them by the hand to bring them out of the land of Egypt, My covenant which they broke, although I was a husband to them," declares the LORD.* **Jeremiah 31:31-32**

Yeshua began His public teaching ministry in the northern areas of Israel. Why didn't He just go to Jerusalem and begin working His ministry there? All the religious leaders and the temple were in Jerusalem. Why did He work His ministry among the less educated and those who intermingled with the unclean Gentiles in and around ten Gentile cities of Decapolis? Some Christian teachers say that the Messiah started His work among the Gentiles since the future Church was going to be predominantly Gentile in nature. This is a significant error in teaching. Everything Yeshua did was to fulfill prophecy about Himself. Yeshua ministered first in Galilee because it was the tribal lands of the tribes of Zebulun and Naphtali (the first tribes that went into captivity because of the Assyrians). He did so because Isaiah's prophecies of the *Greater Exodus* said this was where the Messiah would do the work of consolation and redemption!

> *But there will be no more gloom for her who was in anguish; in earlier times He treated the land of Zebulun and the land of Naphtali with contempt, but later on He shall make it glorious, by the way of the sea, on the other side of Jordan, Galilee of the Gentiles.* **Isaiah 9:1**

The God of Israel judged the House of Israel (the Northern tribes) by allowing the Assyrians to attack and take them captive. This judgment and exile to other nations began first with the Northern kingdom in 722 B.C. The House of Judah (the Southern tribes) was judged much later in 70 A.D. and taken captive by the Romans. In between those two events, the Messiah ministered first to those areas which had gone into exile first, the northern regions of the House of Israel. He came to repair the breach where the breach first occurred. Even the Messiah Himself read from the scroll of Isaiah (Luke 4:17-21) saying that He was the literal fulfillment of the words. To the shock of everyone there at Nazareth, Yeshua stood up to read from Isaiah 61 and then announced that He was the One sent by His (heavenly) Father to free the captives and release prisoners. They were greatly astonished. They knew His (earthly) father was Joseph the carpenter and could not understand that He was speaking as the Son of God, sent by His Father.

> *The Spirit of the Lord GOD is upon me, because the LORD has anointed me to bring good news to the afflicted; He has sent me to bind up the brokenhearted, to proclaim liberty to captives, and freedom to prisoners; to proclaim the favorable year of the LORD...* **Isaiah 61:1-2a**

Yeshua was referring to the Messianic expectation to bring back the exiles. To fulfill another prophecy of being rejected, He spoke this announcement in His hometown and, as prophesied, His hometown brethren rejected His message and He moved His ministry to Capernaum. By the way, Nazareth, and anyone from there, was defined as being "despised." In John 1:46, Nathanael echoes this proverb in his reply to Philip, "Can any good thing come out of Nazareth?"

Before we leave this Isaiah passage read by the Messiah, you should note that He ended His quotation midsentence. He only read the first phrase in the first sentence of Isaiah 61:2. Isaiah did begin describing a single person who is anointed (the Messiah) but then shifted to describing a group of persons who are at the end of the ages. The context of the passage is a mixture of great tribulation and Messianic kingdom issues, as you will see.

> *To proclaim... ,* [Yeshua left off reading here; the passage continues] *and the day of vengeance of our God; to comfort all who mourn, to grant those who mourn in Zion, giving them a garland instead of ashes, the oil of gladness instead of mourning, the mantle of praise instead of a spirit of fainting. So they will be called oaks of righteousness, the planting of the* LORD, *that He may be glorified.*
> **Isaiah 61:2b-3**

Those who proclaim the *day of vengeance* of our God and comfort others are the remnant in the *Greater Exodus*. The *planting of the* LORD is a direct reference to the Olive Tree Israel. One of the definitions of Israel is the *planting of the* LORD. This passage describes the remnant of Israel. He continues on.

> *Instead of your shame you will have a double portion, and instead of humiliation they will shout for joy over their portion. Therefore they will possess a double portion in their land, everlasting joy will be theirs.* **Isaiah 61:7**

## ENDING THE EXILE AND WORKING TOWARD RESTORATION

The transformation from shame and humiliation to everlasting joy is an excellent description of the *Greater Exodus* by the Prophet. However, there should be no more doubt as to who the group is in this prophecy with this final statement.

> *I will rejoice greatly in the* Lord, *My soul will exult in my God; for He has clothed me with garments of salvation, He has wrapped me with a robe of righteousness, as a bridegroom decks himself with a garland, and as a bride adorns herself with her jewels.* **Isaiah 61:10**

These are the words of the remnant of Israel—the Bride of the Messiah—who has prepared herself upon completing the *Greater Exodus*.

The Gospel of Matthew also quotes from Isaiah concerning the tribal lands of Zebulun and Naphtali, the area around Capernaum in the Galilee. Like Nazareth, they heard Yeshua preaching the good news.

> *...and leaving Nazareth, He came and settled in Capernaum, which is by the sea, in the region of Zebulun and Naphtali. This was to fulfill what was spoken through Isaiah the prophet: "The land of Zebulun and the land of Naphtali, by the way of the sea, beyond the Jordan, Galilee of the Gentiles—the people who were sitting in darkness saw a great light, and those who were sitting in the land and shadow of death, upon them a light dawned."*
> **Matthew 4:13-16**

Yeshua knew that many of the House of Israel were still scattered, such as the tribes of Zebulun and Naphtali. He specifically made reference to the exiled flock (the House of Israel) that was already far away when He spoke of Himself as the prophesied Shepherd who will gather ALL the flock of Israel.

# ENDING THE EXILE AND WORKING TOWARD RESTORATION

*I am the good shepherd; and I know My own, and My own know Me, even as the Father knows Me and I know the Father; and I lay down My life for the sheep. I have other sheep, which are not of this fold* [the House of Israel in captivity]; *I must bring them also, and they will hear My voice; and they will become one flock with one shepherd.*
**John 10:14-16**

Yeshua's statement is directly in line with Jeremiah's reference to the Messiah being the Shepherd, the righteous Branch of David. If you will recall, David was a shepherd of his father's flock before he became king of Israel. The Son of David (the Son of God) was to do the same thing but not with small animals called sheep. The *sheep* He was shepherding were the remnant of Israel.

*"Then I Myself will gather the remnant of My flock out of all the countries where I have driven them and bring them back to their pasture, and they will be fruitful and multiply. I will also raise up shepherds over them and they will tend them; and they will not be afraid any longer, nor be terrified, nor will any be missing," declares the LORD. "Behold, the days are coming," declares the LORD, "When I shall raise up for David a righteous Branch; and He will reign as king and act wisely and do justice and righteousness in the land."* **Jeremiah 23:3-5**

Jeremiah then goes on to explain how the exodus led by the Messiah would be greater than the one that came out of Egypt. This is one of two passages where we coin the phrase the "*Greater Exodus.*"

*"Therefore behold, the days are coming," declares the LORD, "when they will no longer say, 'As the LORD lives, who brought up the sons of Israel from the land of Egypt,' but, 'As the LORD lives, who brought up and led back the*

*descendants of the household of Israel from the north land and from all the countries where I had driven them.' Then they will live on their own soil."* **Jeremiah 23:7-8**

This comparison from the Egyptian exodus to the *Greater Exodus* is also found in Jeremiah 16:14-15.

If Christians understood the other prophecies of the Messiah, including the consolation of Israel and the redemption of Jerusalem, they would be able to give a proper answer to Jews denying Yeshua. However, many of them have never heard of the teachings and have no concept of the exodus from Egypt being a prophecy of how God will deliver all of His people from the trauma at the end of days. Still further, many Christians do not see themselves as descendants of Abraham nor being the remnant of Israel. So, these words and promises of God have no bearing on their faith. This is tragic.

In the Book of Romans Chapters 9 through 11, the Apostle Paul defines the remnant of Israel. He clearly states that being a physical descendant does not automatically make you part of the remnant of Israel. He lays out his definition saying:

*That is, it is not the children of the flesh who are children of God, but the children of the promise are regarded as descendants.* **Romans 9:8**

In Romans 11, Paul spoke of native and wild branches being grafted into the olive tree of Israel, which is a reference to the diversity of the children of promise. The fact that the native branches were broken away made it possible for God to include the nations (the believing aliens and sojourners) in His redemption. This goes back to God's promise to Abraham that all *the families of the earth would be blessed.* The term "Gentiles" can mean "nations," but the spiritual connotation is "unbelievers."

## ENDING THE EXILE AND WORKING TOWARD RESTORATION

Paul taught that anyone believing in Yeshua was a true descendant of Abraham (children of promise) and part of the remnant of Israel even though they come from the Gentile nations. The *Greater Exodus* is not limited to the natural born of Israel. It is for the remnant of Israel (the children of promise). All believers of Yeshua the Messiah are part of the remnant of Israel whether they realize it or not; they have ceased to be "Gentiles." Yeshua Himself said as much in commissioning His disciples to minister not to "unbelievers" but to "believers."

> *These twelve Yeshua sent out after instructing them, saying, "Do not go in the way of the Gentiles, and do not enter any city of the Samaritans; but rather go to the lost sheep of the house of Israel."* **Matthew 10:5-6**

Paul concludes the matter in Romans 9 through 11 with "thus all Israel will be saved" as part of his teaching of the *Greater Exodus*.

S E V E N

# THE GREAT TRIBULATION AND THE GREATER EXODUS

One of the most powerful teachings for the end of the ages is the great tribulation and the future judgment of God on the whole earth. Yeshua called it *a great tribulation* (Matthew 24:21), while most of the prophets of Israel refer to the judgments as the *day of the LORD*. Zephaniah, one of the Minor Prophets, focuses almost exclusively on the topic, defining it this way:

> *Near is the great day of the LORD, near and coming very quickly; listen, the day of the LORD! In it the warrior cries out bitterly. A day of wrath is that day, a day of trouble and distress, a day of destruction and desolation, a day of darkness and gloom, a day of clouds and thick darkness, a day of trumpet and battle cry, against the fortified cities and the high corner towers. I will bring distress on men so that they will walk like the blind, because they have sinned against the LORD; and their blood will be poured out like dust, and their flesh like dung. Neither their silver nor their gold will be able to deliver them on the day of the LORD's wrath; and all the earth will be devoured in the fire of His jealousy, for He will make a complete end, indeed a terrifying one, of all the inhabitants of the earth.*
> 
> **Zephaniah 1:14-18**

Zephaniah is not alone in his description of absolute judgment on a specific future day. Isaiah offers a similar description.

*Wail, for the day of the* LORD *is near! It will come as destruction from the Almighty. Therefore all hands will fall limp, and every man's heart will melt. They will be terrified, pains and anguish will take hold of them; they will writhe like a woman in labor, they will look at one another in astonishment, their faces aflame. Behold, the day of the* LORD *is coming, cruel, with fury and burning anger, to make the land a desolation; and He will exterminate its sinners from it. For the stars of heaven and their constellations will not flash forth their light; the sun will be dark when it rises, and the moon will not shed its light. Thus I will punish the world for its evil, and the wicked for their iniquity; I will also put an end to the arrogance of the proud, and abase the haughtiness of the ruthless. I will make mortal man scarcer than pure gold, and mankind than the gold of Ophir. Therefore I shall make the heavens tremble, and the earth will be shaken from its place at the fury of the* LORD *of hosts in the day of His burning anger.* **Isaiah 13:6-13**

Both of these prophets speak of the future *day of the* LORD in absolute terms when describing the severity and comprehensiveness of this future judgment upon sinners. "*He will make a complete end, indeed a terrifying one, of all the inhabitants of the earth* and *I will make mortal man scarcer than pure gold, and mankind than the gold of Ophir.*" The gold of Ophir was the legendary gold of King Solomon. According to legend, there was a single wedge (bar) of gold found. Yes, Solomon's gold mine was prolific but the wedge of Ophir was just a legend. To this day, man does not know where Solomon got his gold, let alone the wedge of Ophir.

The illusion of the golden wedge of Ophir is used by the prophet Isaiah to make a comparison in God's future judgment. Summarized, present day mortal man after the *day of the* LORD will be more of a legend than actually present on the earth.

The obvious question for those who believe in the LORD is a simple one. If God is making mortal man at the *day of the* LORD extinct, then how do we as mortal believers survive and make it to the kingdom? Do we all die and then get picked by God at the resurrection? Do we get raptured out first? These are reasonable questions for a believer to ask. This is the reason why so many end-time prophecy books are written. The writers are trying to answer the question of how do believers escape the absolute judgment of God on His enemies. The answers to these questions are also part of the *Greater Exodus* teaching. Essentially, God is going to deliver us the same way He did the children of Israel from Pharaoh and Egypt. First, let's see what Zephaniah says about our escape from the *day of the* LORD.

> *Gather yourselves together, yes, gather, O nation without shame, before the decree takes effect – the day passes like the chaff – before the burning anger of the* LORD *comes upon you, before the day of the* LORD*'s anger comes upon you. Seek the* LORD*, all you humble of the earth who have carried out His ordinances; seek righteousness, seek humility. Perhaps you will be hidden in the day of the* LORD*'s anger.* **Zephaniah 2:1-3**

The word *perhaps* is not so assuring but it does allude to some kind of escape or protection that involves *gathering*. Zephaniah's allusion is intended to draw us out to fear God and seek His protection and deliverance. Zephaniah later speaks to the *Greater Exodus* directly.

> *Shout for joy, O daughter of Zion! Shout in triumph, O Israel! Rejoice and exult with all your heart, O daughter of Jerusalem! The* LORD *has taken away His judgments*

> *against you, He has cleared away your enemies. The King of Israel, the LORD, is in your midst; you will fear disaster no more. In that day it will be said to Jerusalem: "Do not be afraid, O Zion; do not let your hands fall limp. The LORD your God is in your midst, a victorious warrior. He will exult over you with joy, He will be quiet in His love, He will rejoice over you with shouts of joy." "I will gather those who grieve about the appointed feasts – they came from you, O Zion; the reproach of exile is a burden on them. Behold, I am going to deal at that time with all your oppressors, I will save the lame and gather the outcast, and I will turn their shame into praise and renown in all the earth. At that time I will bring you in, even at the time when I gather you together; indeed, I will give you renown and praise among all the peoples of the earth, when I restore your fortunes before your eyes," says the LORD.*
> **Zephaniah 3:14-20**

Zephaniah uses a powerful technique by speaking the words of God directly to the final generation. At the words, "I will gather you…" we hear the Messiah. Only He has the power to *deal* with our *oppressors* and equally *save the lame and gather the outcast*.

Turning back to Isaiah and his dire definition of the final judgment, we find similar words comforting us concerning the *Greater Exodus*.

> *Now it will come about in that day that the remnant of Israel, and those of the house of Jacob who have escaped, will never again rely on the one who struck them, but will truly rely on the LORD, the Holy One of Israel. A remnant will return, the remnant of Jacob, to the mighty God. For though your people, O Israel, may be like the sand of the sea, only a remnant within them will return; a destruc-*

*tion is determined, overflowing with righteousness. For a complete destruction, one that is decreed, the Lord GOD of hosts will execute in the midst of the whole land.*
***Isaiah 10:20-23***

Isaiah's reference to *the remnant of Israel, and those of the house of Jacob* is a reference to those in the land and outside the land of Israel. It is not an absolute, but most of the prophets use this distinction of Israel vs. Jacob as a reference of where the people of God are located, whether in the land or outside the land. Isaiah also uses the phrase *complete destruction, one that is decreed* as a reference to the *day of the LORD*. The return of the remnant is a reference to those in the *Greater Exodus* who are able to escape and survive the *day of the LORD*. Isaiah then follows these words with specific emphasis on the *Greater Exodus* as compared to the exodus out of Egypt.

*Then it will happen on that day that the LORD will again recover the second time with His hand the remnant of His people, who will remain, from Assyria, Egypt, Pathros, Cush, Elam, Shinar, Hamath, and from the islands of the sea. And He will lift up a standard for the nations, and will assemble the banished ones of Israel, and will gather the dispersed of Judah from the four corners of the earth. Then the jealousy of Ephraim will depart, and those who harass Judah will be cut off; Ephraim will not be jealous of Judah, and Judah will not harass Ephraim. And they will swoop down on the slopes of the Philistines on the west; together they will plunder the sons of the east; they will possess Edom and Moab; and the sons of Ammon will be subject to them. And the LORD will utterly destroy the tongue of the Sea of Egypt; and He will wave His hand over the River with His scorching wind; and He will strike it into seven streams, and make men walk over dry-shod. And there will be a highway from Assyria for the remnant*

*of His people who will be left, just as there was for Israel in the day that they came up out of the land of Egypt.*
**Isaiah 11:11-16**

The final expression of this passage relates back to the exodus, but it is clear here that the *Greater Exodus* is related in purpose and timing to the final judgment called the *day of the* LORD. Isaiah expresses the final judgment in parallel fashion with the gathering and deliverance of Zion.

*For the* LORD *has a day of vengeance, a year of recompense for the cause of Zion.* **Isaiah 34:8**

The prophet Joel adds another voice that defines the *day of the* LORD three distinct times and then alludes to an exodus the final time.

*Alas for the day! For the day of the* LORD *is near, and it will come as destruction from the Almighty.* **Joel 1:15**

*Blow a trumpet in Zion, and sound an alarm on My holy mountain! Let all the inhabitants of the land tremble, for the day of the* LORD *is coming; surely it is near, ...* **Joel 2:1**

*I will display wonders in the sky and on the earth, blood, fire, and columns of smoke. The sun will be turned into darkness and the moon into blood before the great and awesome day of the* LORD *comes. And it will come about that whoever calls on the name of the* LORD *will be delivered; for on Mount Zion and in Jerusalem there will be those who escape, as the* LORD *has said, even among the survivors whom the* LORD *calls.* **Joel 2:30-32**

Those who call upon the LORD are those looking to the Messiah (the leader of the *Greater Exodus*), and those who escape (they are *called* survivors) are also the "remnant" of Israel (those who remain and are sustained by the Lord).

According to the end-time prophetic scenario given by the Messiah, the *day of the Lord* is the conclusion of the great tribulation (the final 3½ years). See the diagram for the Tribulation Timeline in Appendix A. But what starts the great tribulation? Yeshua reminded us that the great tribulation would actually begin with the *Abomination of Desolation*, a prophecy given by the prophet Daniel (Daniel 12:1b). The Abomination of Desolation consists of two events: the shutting down of an operating altar on the temple mount in Jerusalem and the setting up of an image of the antimessiah on that mount. The great tribulation then lasts 3½ years and is followed by "*the days immediately following the tribulation of those days.*" It is in those days immediately after that the fall feasts occur and the *day of the Lord* (Yom Kippur) is fulfilled. So, what feast is at the beginning of the 3½ year tribulation? Answer: Passover and the Feast of Unleavened Bread. When did the exodus from Egypt begin? Answer: At the same time. When will the *Greater Exodus* begin? Answer: At Passover. The history of the exodus given by Moses gives us the base pattern for the future *Greater Exodus*.

The *Greater Exodus* begins at the start of the great tribulation with the Messiah leading His flock to safety by following His words to escape at the signs of the "Abomination of Desolation" and concludes with the Messiah's triumphant return to Jerusalem with us as He promised. For believers to escape, survive, and endure the great tribulation, God's deliverance must extend throughout the great tribulation. Like the exodus out of Egypt, the *Greater Exodus* is the gathering and leading of God's people away from the places of danger and judgment during the great tribulation.

Just as the *day of the Lord* has been described in dire terms, so is the great tribulation. In the exodus, God inflicted ten different judgments upon Egypt before the exodus began. For the future exodus, the exodus begins after the signs of the Abomination of Desolation (which occur just before a future Passover) and is followed by a series of seals, trumpets, and plagues. Therefore, many of the prophets speak of the tribulation and the *day of the LORD* together. Interestingly, the Hebrew word for "tribulations" is *Mitzrayim*. This is also the Hebrew name for Egypt. Coming out of Egypt is coming out of *tribulations*. Thus, coming out of the nations (the world system) during the great tribulation is compared to coming out of "Egypt."

The great tribulation judgments will overwhelm the world and will include such things as shortages of basic resources, wars being waged, and people being plagued by many diseases. No matter how you do the math, the prophecies speak of half the world's population dying in those days. The fourth seal speaks of one-fourth of mankind dying.

> *I looked, and behold, an ashen horse; and he who sat on it had the name Death; and Hades was following with him. Authority was given to them over a fourth of the earth, to kill with sword and with famine and with pestilence and by the wild beasts of the earth.* **Revelation 6:8**

Then the sixth trumpet speaks of one third of mankind suffering death.

> *A third of mankind was killed by these three plagues, by the fire and the smoke and the brimstone, which proceeded out of their mouths.* **Revelation 9:18**

As of 8/28/2013, at 1:30pm, the world's population was about 7,175,231,619 and it has increased from there daily. Using the numbers from August 2013, if we were to lose one-fourth of the world's population, that equates to 1,793,807,905 who would perish during the fourth seal, leaving 5,381,423,714. If one-third of those remaining are then killed by Revelation 9:18—that is another 1,775,869,826 who would die with only 3,605,553,888 remaining. This remaining number is nearly one-half the original number of 7,175,231,619. I used these actual numbers to give a real perspective. Here are the same numbers in list form.

| | |
|---|---:|
| Population (August 2013) | 7,175,231,619 |
| One fourth killed | - 1,793,807,904 |
| remaining population | 5,381,423,714 |
| One third killed | - 1,775,869,825 |
| remaining population | 3,605,553,888 |

When we speak of past wars and diseases we speak in millions of people. The prophecies of the great tribulation speak of its judgments in billions of people. Truly, the great tribulation is to be a time of distress as the world has never seen before.

> *And there will be a time of distress such as never occurred since there was a nation until that time; and at that time your people, everyone who is found written in the book, will be rescued.* **Daniel 12:1b**

But how will God rescue His people in the midst of a world that is distressed beyond anything history has ever seen? Part of the answer is embedded in the judgment of the fourth seal where one-fourth of mankind dies.

This judgment details four elements: sword (warfare and violence), famine (starvation), pestilence (insects and disease), and wild beasts. The prophet Ezekiel first spoke of these same four elements of judgment but ended with an incredible message of comfort for the future. Let's see how Ezekiel accomplishes this.

> *"Son of man, if a country sins against Me by committing unfaithfulness, and I stretch out My hand against it, destroy its supply of bread, send famine against it and cut off from it both man and beast, even though these three men, Noah, Daniel and Job were in its midst, by their own righteousness they could only deliver themselves," declares the Lord G*OD*.* **Ezekiel 14:13-14**

Ezekiel refers to Noah, Daniel, and Job as men who have been previously delivered from judgments. Noah was delivered from God's worldwide judgment of the flood. Daniel was delivered from the judgment of a king (man). Job was delivered by the LORD from oppression and great loss at the hand of Satan. They stand as examples of deliverance. The LORD has said through Ezekiel that if He puts a judgment of a famine upon a nation that only Noah, Daniel, and Job could be delivered if they were there. He repeats this comparison for the judgment of wild beasts and adds some degree as to how exclusive the deliverance would be for the three. Even their families and children would not be delivered.

> *"...though these three men were in its midst, as I live," declares the Lord G*OD*, "they could not deliver either their sons or their daughters. They alone would be delivered, but the country would be desolate."* **Ezekiel 14:16**

Then Ezekiel repeats this comparison again for the judgment of the sword and finally presents the same comparison for the judgment of plague (pestilence and disease). Again, he repeats the conclusion that only Noah, Daniel, and Job would be delivered by themselves.

> *"They would deliver only themselves by their righteousness."*
> **Ezekiel 14:20**

Then, to add emphasis to God's argument, a question is posed.

## THE GREAT TRIBULATION AND THE GREATER EXODUS

*For thus says the Lord G*OD*, "How much more when I send My four severe judgments against Jerusalem: sword, famine, wild beasts, and plague to cut off man and beast from it!"* **Ezekiel 14:21**

What if all four judgments were to fall at the same time? Wait! This is the judgment of the fourth seal in Revelation. Would we expect any different result? The obvious answer is no. But then Ezekiel speaks of a deliverance and a comfort that is exclusive to the prophecies of the *Greater Exodus*.

*"Yet, behold, survivors will be left in it who will be brought out, both sons and daughters. Behold, they are going to come forth to you and you will see their conduct and actions; then you will be comforted for the calamity which I have brought against Jerusalem for everything which I have brought upon it. Then they will comfort you when you see their conduct and actions, for you will know that I have not done in vain whatever I did to it," declares the Lord G*OD*.* **Ezekiel 14:22-23**

Care and concern for children is more powerful than self-survival for parents. Remember the children of Israel entering the land the first time fearing for their children? That fear will be palpable in the great tribulation for parents. The deliverance promised in the *Greater Exodus* addresses this fear directly. Not only is there to be deliverance offered to the tribulation saints (those who are part of the *Greater Exodus*) beyond Noah, Daniel, and Job, but that deliverance is extended to their sons and daughters. What group of potential survivors could possibly be greater than the testimonies of Noah, Daniel, and Job? This is the answer for the fourth seal judgment in the great tribulation, but what about all of the other judgments of the great tribulation? Who is able to stand in the midst of ALL the tribulation judgments? That question is posed and answered in the Book of Revelation.

# THE GREAT TRIBULATION AND THE GREATER EXODUS

# EIGHT

# WHO IS ABLE TO STAND IN THAT DAY?

The Book of Revelation is commonly called the Apocalypse. It is filled with drama, symbolism, and spiritual scenery. It also describes the incredible judgment of God upon the whole world and poses the following question: "Who is able to stand in the day of the wrath of the Lamb?" (Revelation 6:17). The question could have just as easily been asked, "Who will escape in the great tribulation and be part of the *Greater Exodus*?" The answer to both questions is the same. As quickly as it asks the question, Revelation Chapter 7 answers the question.

Those who are able to stand after the *day of the* LORD are the same believers who survive the 3½ year great tribulation. They are divided into two groups: the sealed 144,000 special bond-servants of the LORD representing the 12 listed tribes of Israel and the "innumerable" tribulation saints. The numbers here are surprising because the natural tendency is to expect the number of survivors to be low or minimal. But instead, the salvation of God will be gloriously exhibited by saving more people than anyone would expect. I believe the number will be greater than all those "saved" since the creation. Let's address the first group:

> *And I heard the number of those who were sealed, one hundred and forty-four thousand sealed from every tribe of the sons of Israel:* **Revelation 7:4**

## WHO IS ABLE TO STAND IN THAT DAY?

Revelation goes on to number 12,000 sealed from each of the named tribes. The seal is a visible mark in their foreheads that bears the name of God. They are the ones who will carry out God's deliverance and comfort the people who are escaping. There is something very subtle in this description of the 144,000. To accomplish this particular accounting of Israel, logic says that the two houses of Israel (Judah and Israel) must be re-united! This uniting was also spoken of by the prophet Ezekiel. Ezekiel spoke of a vision of dry bones coming together at the end of the ages (Ezekiel 37:1-6). We know this is a prophecy of Israel at the end of the ages because He precedes the vision with this first.

*$^{24}$For I will take you from the nations, gather you from all the lands, and bring you into your own land.... $^{26}$Moreover, I will give you a new heart and put a new spirit within you; and I will remove the heart of stone from your flesh and give you a heart of flesh. $^{27}$I will put My Spirit within you and cause you to walk in My statutes, and you will be careful to observe My ordinances. $^{28}$You will live in the land that I gave to your forefathers; so you will be My people, and I will be your God.*
**Ezekiel 36:24, 26-28**

Ezekiel then goes on to specifically explain the re-union of the two houses of Israel as a part of the *Greater Exodus.*

*And you, son of man, take for yourself one stick and write on it, 'For Judah and for the sons of Israel, his companions'; then take another stick and write on it, 'For Joseph, the stick of Ephraim and all the house of Israel, his companions.' Then join them for yourself one to another into one stick, that they may become one in your hand. When the sons of your people speak to you saying, "Will you not declare to us what you mean by these?" say to them, "Thus*

## WHO IS ABLE TO STAND IN THAT DAY?

*says the Lord GOD, 'Behold, I will take the stick of Joseph, which is in the hand of Ephraim, and the tribes of Israel, his companions; and I will put them with it, with the stick of Judah, and make them one stick, and they will be one in My hand.'"* **Ezekiel 37:16-19**

Should there be any lingering doubt that the reunion of the two houses of Israel is part of the *Greater Exodus* and essential to the sealing of the 144,000 in the great tribulation, Ezekiel seems to erase it altogether.

*The sticks on which you write will be in your hand before their eyes. Say to them, "Thus says the Lord GOD, 'Behold, I will take the sons of Israel from among the nations where they have gone, and I will gather them from every side and bring them into their own land; and I will make them one nation in the land, on the mountains of Israel; and one king will be king for all of them; and they will no longer be two nations, and no longer be divided into two kingdoms. They will no longer defile themselves with their idols, or with their detestable things, or with any of their transgressions; but I will deliver them from all their dwelling places in which they have sinned, and will cleanse them. And they will be My people, and I will be their God.'"*
**Ezekiel 37:20-23**

The sealing of the 144,000 proves that the two houses of Israel have been united and that all twelve tribes are present and recognized as such. As you can imagine, the antichrist in the great tribulation will hate this. He will do his best to break this union of Israel, nevertheless he will fail.

*Then I* [the false shepherd (antichrist)] *cut my second staff, Union, in pieces, to break the brotherhood between Judah and Israel.* **Zechariah 11:14**

## WHO IS ABLE TO STAND IN THAT DAY?

The other group listed in Revelation 7 is called the tribulation saints. They will literally take refuge in the name of the LORD by standing with the 144,000 who have God's name written on their foreheads. The 144,000 do not die in the great tribulation. They are empowered to deliver the tribulation saints. Finally, they are the special welcoming committee for the Messiah Himself at the temple mount in Jerusalem.

*Then I looked, and behold, the Lamb was standing on Mount Zion, and with Him one hundred and forty-four thousand, having His name and the name of His Father written on their foreheads.* **Revelation 14:1**

As incredible as that seems, there is a parallel story in the Egyptian exodus that foretells about the survival and protection of the 144,000. Toward the end of the wilderness journey, the children of Israel began to move north in preparation to cross the Jordan. Then, they encountered the Moabite king Balak, the prophet Baalam, and five Midianite kings. Balak mustered the Midianites to join him to oppose Israel. He also hired the prophet Baalam to curse Israel. In the end, Baalam was not successful in cursing Israel but instead counseled the Midianites how to harm Israel by seducing Israel away from Moses and God. Twenty-four thousand sons of Israel died as a result. God then directed Moses to assemble a force of 12,000 warriors (1,000 from each tribe) to battle the Midianites and kill Balaam. But here is the real story. Not one of the 12,000 died in their victory over the Midianites! (Numbers 31:48-49) In the same way, the 144,000 (12,000 from each tribe) will defend the remnant from harm and not one of them will suffer death.

Just how many saints will be delivered by the efforts of the 144,000? That answer is also given.

*After these things I looked, and behold, a great multitude which no one could count, from every nation and all tribes*

> *and peoples and tongues, standing before the throne and before the Lamb, clothed in white robes, and palm branches were in their hands; and they cry out with a loud voice, saying, "Salvation to our God who sits on the throne, and to the Lamb."* **Revelation 7:9-10**

There are many things seen in the Book of Revelation that are numbered, from day counts to the size of groups, but this assembly could not be numbered by any man. Aside from the great number, this group is observed waving palm branches. Traditionally, these leafy branches are part of the Feast of Tabernacles (coverings for their Sukkot shelters). You may recall that when Yeshua entered Jerusalem for the last time the people were waving palm branches. This was stunning because they were still celebrating the previous Feast of Tabernacles based on what Yeshua had said (John 7:37) and wanting to herald Him as king. Remember, He was arrested for being a king of the people. The religious leaders used this against Him in His trial before Pilate. However, Yeshua entered Jerusalem to do the work of the Lamb of God (redemption). Later, at the end the ages, He will enter Jerusalem as the King to celebrate Sukkot (Tabernacles). This is why the tribulation saints wave their branches. They are preparing for the Feast of Tabernacles (the first feast of the kingdom) as prophesied by Zechariah.

> *Then it will come about that any who are left of all the nations* [the believing remnant] *that went against Jerusalem will go up from year to year to worship the King, the LORD of hosts, and to celebrate the Feast of Booths* [Tabernacles]. **Zechariah 14:16**

The Book of Revelation describes the tribulation saints further.

> *These are the ones who come out of the great tribulation, and they have washed their robes and made them white*

> *in the blood of the Lamb. For this reason, they are before the throne of God; and they serve Him day and night in His temple; and He who sits on the throne will spread His tabernacle over them. They will hunger no longer, nor thirst anymore; nor will the sun beat down on them, nor any heat; for the Lamb in the center of the throne will be their shepherd, and will guide them to springs of the water of life; and God will wipe every tear from their eyes.*
> **Revelation 7:14b-17**

Consider what the tribulation saints will endure during the *Greater Exodus*. They will face hunger, thirst, and the heat of the sun. The prophet Isaiah speaks of this threat and God's deliverance specifically.

> *They will not hunger or thirst, nor will the scorching heat or sun strike them down; for He who has compassion on them will lead them, and will guide them to springs of water.*
> **Isaiah 49:10**

The great tribulation is not going to be convenient or easy. The same can be said for the *Greater Exodus* of believers. There will be struggles, just as our ancestors faced when they left Egypt. These struggles were not just from the environment of the wilderness. God purposely caused them to suffer hunger and thirst. God was testing them and trying to transform them from slaves to free men. The same will happen to the believers in the *Greater Exodus*. They will be tested and transformed from mortals to immortals.

> *You shall remember all the way which the Lord your God has led you in the wilderness these forty years, that He might humble you, testing you, to know what was in your heart, whether you would keep His commandments or not. He humbled you and let you be hungry, and fed you with*

> *manna which you did not know, nor did your fathers know, that He might make you understand that man does not live by bread alone, but man lives by everything that proceeds out of the mouth of the LORD.* **Deuteronomy 8:2-3**

God gave our ancestors water from the Rock and manna for bread, which appeared each day like the dew (except on Sabbath). God has also promised the basics of life for those who are part of the *Greater Exodus*. By the way, the Book of Revelation also refers to the tribulation saints as *overcomers* in chapters 2 and 3. The Messiah has given a series of seven messages, many with correction, to prepare His people to be overcomers of the coming things. The Messiah has promised manna again and water to drink when the world will struggle for those basics.

> *To him who overcomes, to him I will give some of the hidden manna, and I will give him a white stone, and a new name written on the stone which no one knows but he who receives it.* **Revelation 2:17b**

The white stone can be translated as the "brightly illuminated" instead of "white." This appears to be a reference back to the Urim and Thummim, the stones of determination in the Ephod of the High Priest. The overcomers are affirmed in their identity as the remnant of Israel by these stones.

The great tribulation will be a 3½ year period beginning in the season of winter and concluding in the season of summer, just before the biblical appointed times of Trumpets, Atonement, and Tabernacles (see the Tribulation Timeline, Appendix A). The *Greater Exodus* will be God's method of deliverance for this time period through the leadership of the 144,000 in the various escaping camps. Those who are delivered will dwell in mobile shelters (sukkot). The Psalmist says it best.

## WHO IS ABLE TO STAND IN THAT DAY?

> *You will not be afraid of the terror by night, or of the arrow that flies by day; of the pestilence that stalks in darkness, or of the destruction that lays waste at noon. A thousand may fall at your side and ten thousand at your right hand; but it shall not approach you. You will only look on with your eyes, and see the recompense of the wicked. For you have made the LORD, my refuge, even the Most High, your dwelling place. No evil will befall you, nor will any plague come near your tent* [shelter/sukkah]. ***Psalm 91:5-10***

Where will they go? When Israel left Egypt they went to the wilderness. The prophets say the same will happen for those believers who escape from their homes, cities, and countries; however, it is called the "*wilderness of the peoples,*" literally meaning "people will be out of the cities" in the various nations.

> *"As I live," declares the Lord GOD, "surely with a mighty hand and with an outstretched arm and with wrath poured out, I shall be king over you. I will bring you out from the peoples and gather you from the lands where you are scattered, with a mighty hand and with an outstretched arm and with wrath poured out; and I will bring you into the wilderness of the peoples, and there I will enter into judgment with you face to face. As I entered into judgment with your fathers in the wilderness of the land of Egypt, so I will enter into judgment with you," declares the Lord GOD. I will make you pass under the rod, and I will bring you into the bond of the covenant; and I will purge from you the rebels and those who transgress against Me; I will bring them out of the land where they sojourn, but they will not enter the land of Israel. Thus you will know that I am the LORD."*
> ***Ezekiel 20:33-38***

This is one of the most dramatic and explicit descriptions of the *Greater Exodus* using the very language that God used in bringing the children of Israel out of Egypt. God directly compares the *Greater Exodus* (the *"wilderness of the peoples"*) to the exodus, speaking of His judgments upon the world and rendering judgment upon those in the camp who will rebel (as He did with Korah, Dathan, and Abiram in Numbers 16 of the exodus). Even God's purpose remains the same for the *Greater Exodus* as with the exodus: *Thus you will know that I am the* LORD.

The Book of Revelation also describes two individuals who will also play a role in addition to the two groups of the 144,000 bond-servants and tribulation saints. They are not specifically identified, but consensus among Bible Scholars holds that they are Moses and Elijah re-incarnate or those in the *spirit* of Moses and Elijah. What is profound about them is not who they might be but instead what they do. They announce the tribulation judgments from God to the world.

> *And I will grant authority to my two witnesses, and they will prophesy for twelve hundred and sixty days, clothed in sackcloth. These are the two olive trees and the two lampstands that stand before the Lord of the earth. And if anyone desires to harm them, fire proceeds out of their mouth and devours their enemies; and if anyone would desire to harm them, in this manner he must be killed. These have the power to shut up the sky, in order that rain may not fall during the days of their prophesying; and they have power over the waters to turn them into blood, and to smite the earth with every plague, as often as they desire.*
> **Revelation 11:3-6**

This prophecy tracks with the exodus as well. Moses and Aaron were the two witnesses before Pharaoh. They warned Pharaoh and the Egyptians and then introduced the judgments of God upon Egypt. There is a striking pattern in the ten judgments that fell on Egypt. The first can be subdivided into three sets. This pattern is visible based on the location of the judgment announcement by Moses and Aaron. The three sets of judgments were presented first at the river Nile, then at the palace, and finally they were unannounced. Only the final judgment, the death of the firstborn, does not conform to this pattern, setting it apart from the others. The same peculiarity is true of the great tribulation. However, it is much more visible. There are three sets of seven judgments (the seals, trumpets, and plagues) followed by the *day of the* LORD. Just as Moses and Aaron introduced these judgments to Pharaoh and Egypt, it appears that two witnesses will announce the judgments to the antimessiah and the world. The prophecy of the two witnesses says that they will do this during all the days of the 3½ year great tribulation, only to be killed and bodily resurrected in the days immediately following it.

The Torah teaches that you must have two or three witnesses to establish truth, thus the witness of Moses and Aaron to Egypt established the truth of God's message in that day. Some have argued that the judgments that fell on Egypt occurred naturally and were not by the hand of God but they forget that Moses and Aaron announced them beforehand. This proved that the judgment was by God's hand. The same will likely happen in the great tribulation. God will likely use natural and providential elements in his judgments. But when the two witnesses speak to the judgment precisely beforehand, it will establish the truth of the matter. The two witnesses will testify to God's judgments upon the earth, even though they may have natural explanations.

The Book of Revelation also describes the *Greater Exodus* by comparing Israel and the remnant as a woman fleeing into the wilderness. It is a picture of remnant Israel escaping the great tribulation.

> *And a great sign appeared in heaven: a woman clothed with the sun, and the moon under her feet, and on her head a crown of twelve stars; and she was with child; and she*

> *cried out, being in labor and in pain to give birth. And another sign appeared in heaven: and behold, a great red dragon having seven heads and ten horns, and on his heads were seven diadems. And his tail swept away a third of the stars of heaven, and threw them to the earth. And the dragon stood before the woman who was about to give birth, so that when she gave birth he might devour her child. And she gave birth to a son, a male child, who is to rule all the nations with a rod of iron; and her child was caught up to God and to His throne. And the woman fled into the wilderness where she had a place prepared by God, so that there she might be nourished for one thousand two hundred and sixty days.* **Revelation 12:1-6**

This description of the woman is a depiction of Israel bringing forth the Messiah with the devil on the attack. The child is the Messiah who will rule all nations with a rod of iron. Then it describes how Israel will escape at the end (like an exodus into the wilderness) and be protected for 1,260 days, which is the same length of days given for the two witnesses.

Yeshua spoke of this prophecy just as Zechariah (Zechariah 14:5) did, indicating that those in Judea (the area surrounding Jerusalem) would have to escape into the wilderness when the Abomination of Desolation was set up. By the way, this is the same place where the scapegoat (the escaping goat) is taken on the Day of Atonement (Yom Kippur). This is the secondary event of the Abomination of Desolation that began the day count of the great tribulation; therefore, the *Greater Exodus* begins with the start of the great tribulation. The bulk of the tribulation saints, those scattered in the nations, will escape to the "*wilderness of the peoples*" at the Passover that immediately follows (they will be only days apart).

[15]*Therefore when you see the abomination of desolation which was spoken of through Daniel the prophet, stand-*

> ing in the holy place (let the reader understand), <sup>16</sup>then let those who are in Judea flee to the mountains;... <sup>20</sup>But pray that your flight may not be in the winter, or on a Sabbath. <sup>21</sup>For then there will be a great tribulation, such as has not occurred since the beginning of the world until now, nor ever shall. **Matthew 24:15-16, 20-21**

Yeshua describes this flight from Judea as a literal emergency with no time to gather other items. Based on Yeshua's description, it is not readily apparent why there is need for such an emergency escape, but the explanation is found in the Revelation prophecy with the woman escaping.

> And when the dragon saw that he was thrown down to the earth, he persecuted the woman who gave birth to the male child. And the two wings of the great eagle were given to the woman, in order that she might fly into the wilderness to her place, where she was nourished for a time and times and half a time, from the presence of the serpent. And the serpent poured water like a river out of his mouth after the woman, so that he might cause her to be swept away with the flood. And the earth helped the woman, and the earth opened its mouth and drank up the river which the dragon poured out of his mouth. And the dragon was enraged with the woman, and went off to make war with the rest of her offspring, who keep the commandments of God and hold to the testimony of Yeshua. **Revelation 12:13-17**

A sudden flash flood in the Judean hills and mountains is the reason for the sudden escape. By the way, flash-flooding in the springtime is a common and deadly occurrence in the Holy Land east of Jerusalem. Apparently, this is the first element of protection prophesied for the *Greater Exodus*. This actually parallels the crossing of the Red Sea and Israel's dramatic deliverance. The crossing of the Red Sea was God's salvation made visible.

## WHO IS ABLE TO STAND IN THAT DAY?

But in the *Greater Exodus*, God opens the earth to swallow a deluge of flood instead of parting the waters.

We cannot leave this passage without noting the phrase *"The wings of the great eagle."* It is a direct reference to the exodus! Moses used this very word picture to describe the exodus out of Egypt.

*Like an eagle that stirs up its nest, that hovers over its young, He spread His wings and caught them [Israel], He carried them on His pinions.* **Deuteronomy 32:11**

When the Book of Revelation says that the dragon goes off to make war with the rest of Israel's offspring, it is referring to the tribulation saints scattered elsewhere in the world during the great tribulation. Where do those fleeing Judea and the deluge go? The only description we have is into the wilderness to her place. Obviously, God will have prepared a place for them to escape the great tribulation. Some have suggested that the place could be Petra, a famous place in Jordan that Israel used to prepare entry into the land. I tend to think that they will make it back to the base of Mount Sinai in Arabia. Regardless of where it is, they will return to the land in the way and manner God purposed in the exodus, with faith in God's provision, protection, and promises.

Finally, the Book of Revelation describes a set of two harvests. The first is a harvest unto God's kingdom while the latter is a harvest unto God's judgment. The first harvest is described this way.

*And I looked, and behold, a white cloud, and sitting on the cloud was one like a son of man, having a golden crown on His head, and a sharp sickle in His hand. And another angel came out of the temple, crying out with a loud voice*

> *to Him who sat on the cloud, "Put in your sickle and reap, because the hour to reap has come, because the harvest of the earth is ripe." And He who sat on the cloud swung His sickle over the earth; and the earth was reaped.*
>
> ***Revelation 14:14-16***

This is a simplified description of the *Greater Exodus* with the "gathering" of the saints from the nations and the final rapture/resurrection. The LORD has said that He will return with all of His saints. This must include the saints of old—those who have passed. They are gathered first and immediately followed by the remaining tribulation saints. This is pictured in the Feast of Trumpets ten days prior to the Day of Atonement. The wrath of God (the second harvest) is not planned for them. This is not such a strange word picture for us. Yeshua spoke of a harvest of wheat and tares. The good grain was gathered up and separated from the tares which were gathered and burned.

The *second harvest* is definitely the wrath of God as described.

> *And another angel came out of the temple which is in heaven, and he also had a sharp sickle. Then another angel, the one who has power over fire, came out from the altar; and he called with a loud voice to him who had the sharp sickle, saying, "Put in your sharp sickle and gather the clusters from the vine of the earth, because her grapes are ripe." So the angel swung his sickle to the earth, and gathered the clusters from the vine of the earth, and threw them into the great wine press of the wrath of God.*
>
> ***Revelation 14:17-19***

**NINE**

# COMPARING THE FUTURE WITH THE ANCIENT PAST

If you believe that God delivered the children of Israel out of Egypt, then you must believe that God will save His people at the end of the age. Either you believe what God has said or you don't. With regard to the salvation and deliverance of God's people at the end of the ages, the Scriptures succinctly say that the remnant of Israel (the House of Jacob) will be saved.

> *Alas! for that day is great, there is none like it; and it is the time of Jacob's distress, but he will be saved from it.*
> **Jeremiah 30:7**

God does not change. God is not a man who does impulsive things. He describes His own character as One who plans, and then does what He has planned. It may not be to the timetable of a man, but it will happen as He said. Isaiah records God's own definition of Himself.

> *Remember the former things long past, for I am God, and there is no other; I am God, and there is no one like Me, declaring the end from the beginning and from ancient times things which have not been done, saying, "My purpose will be established, and I will accomplish all My good pleasure; calling a bird of prey from the east, the man of*

## COMPARING THE FUTURE WITH THE ANCIENT PAST

*My purpose from a far country. Truly I have spoken; truly I will bring it to pass. I have planned it, surely I will do it."*
**Isaiah 46:9-11**

When prophesying of the *Greater Exodus*, the prophets of Israel hold to this powerful characteristic of God and make profound and direct comparisons to the exodus from Egypt. They teach that God had accomplished certain things in the past—in the beginning—that forms the plan of the future. The key to properly understanding the future is to remember the former things long past. Essentially, all of the prophets of Israel agree with this point, but the prophets Jeremiah and Ezekiel emphasize it. Of the two, Jeremiah's comparison of the exodus to the future exodus is expressed in the superlative. It is beyond merely a repeated pattern. He stresses that the word *exodus* won't even evoke the memory of ancient Egypt due to the overwhelming activities of the *Greater Exodus*. I have used the adjective *greater* in this treatise to highlight Jeremiah's superlative comparison.

*"Therefore behold, days are coming," declares the LORD, "when it will no longer be said, 'As the LORD lives, who brought up the sons of Israel out of the land of Egypt,' but, 'As the LORD lives, who brought up the sons of Israel from the land of the north and from all the countries where He had banished them.' For I will restore them to their own land which I gave to their fathers. Behold, I am going to send for many fishermen," declares the LORD, "and they will fish for them; and afterwards I will send for many hunters, and they will hunt them from every mountain and every hill, and from the clefts of the rocks."*
**Jeremiah 16:14-16**

Jeremiah argues that the future exodus from all of the countries (as opposed to only Egypt) constitutes the profundity of not even thinking of Egypt when the word *exodus* is said in the context of the future. We also should note that the reference to *fishermen* takes us back to statements made by Yeshua to Peter after His resurrection. He stated that those proclaiming Him and the "good news" would be "fishers of men." But who are the "hunters" that Jeremiah refers to? Some teachers have suggested that this is a negative element, tracing back to Esau and the ancient conflict with Jacob, and that it hints of Israel being pursued in the last age to their harm. On the contrary, I favor a larger definition for the scale of the Gospel.

Ephraim and the leader of the House of Israel were blessed by Jacob in a special way. If you will recall, Joseph brought his sons Manasseh and Ephraim to Jacob before his death. Despite Ephraim being the younger, Jacob crossed his arms, placing his right hand upon him for the blessing of the firstborn! He then blessed Ephraim to be especially fruitful to the extent that he would be spread worldwide, becoming a part of many nations (Genesis 48:16) and a multitude of nations (Genesis 48:19). The blessing of Moses upon the tribe of Ephraim is just as prolific and keyed to Jacob's previous blessing, but hinting at something very special at the end of the ages.

> *As the firstborn of his ox, majesty is his, and his horns are the horns of the wild ox; with them he shall push the peoples, all at once, to the ends of the earth. And those are the ten thousands of Ephraim, and those are the thousands of Manasseh.* **Deuteronomy 33:17**

Why do we take note of these blessings at the *ends of the earth*? Because this is the language of the *Greater Exodus* with the "fullness of the gentiles." Ephraim is to be the dominant tribe and people gathered out of the nations.

With that said, consider the sea and how many different nations it contacts. The sea touches every continent and many coastlands, hence "fishers of men" will reach them. However, there are nations in the interior of those continents not bordered by the sea. You need "hunters," or those who travel by land, to reach them. Therefore, God's pledge to fish for them and to hunt for them covers the globe, to the *ends of the earth.*

We would be remiss to not speak for a moment about what Jeremiah said and who he was speaking to before declaring the *Greater Exodus*. Jeremiah is speaking directly to the last generation!

> *Now when you tell this people all these words that they will say to you, "For what reason has the* Lord *declared all this great calamity against us? And what is our iniquity, or what is our sin which we have committed against the* Lord *our God?" Then you are to say to them, "It is because your forefathers have forsaken Me," declares the* Lord, *"and have followed other gods and served them and bowed down to them; but Me they have forsaken and have not kept My law. You too have done evil, even more than your forefathers; for behold, you are each one walking according to the stubbornness of his own evil heart, without listening to Me. So I will hurl you out of this land into the land which you have not known, neither you nor your fathers; and there you will serve other gods day and night, for I shall grant you no favor."* **Jeremiah 16:10-13**

This is an amazing piece of literature with Jeremiah of old having a future conversation with the last generation. The calamity being addressed is the worldwide dispersion of Israel due to the sins of the fathers. But it is not just the fathers who are scorned. Jeremiah expressly confronts the last generation, saying their sins are even worse than the ancient fathers. He emphatically states that the last generation is still scattered and still serving other gods with no favor from God. That pretty much sums up the world today.

## COMPARING THE FUTURE WITH THE ANCIENT PAST

Immediately after confronting us in these days, he proclaims the *Greater Exodus* to come (vs 14-16). Now look at the following passage.

> *"For My eyes are on all their ways; they are not hidden from My face, nor is their iniquity concealed from My eyes. I will first doubly repay their iniquity and their sin, because they have polluted My land; they have filled My inheritance with the carcasses of their detestable idols and with their abominations." O LORD, my strength and my stronghold, and my refuge in the day of distress, to You the nations will come from the ends of the earth and say, "Our fathers have inherited nothing but falsehood, futility and things of no profit." Can man make gods for himself? Yet they are not gods! "Therefore behold, I am going to make them know—this time I will make them know My power and My might; and they shall know that My name is the LORD."* **Jeremiah 16:17-21**

Israel's exile to the nations was payment (punishment) for not fulfilling their word in the covenant with God. But the day is coming when the final generation in exile will make God their refuge *in the day of distress*. The remnant of Israel will confess that they have been following *falsehood, futility and things of no profit*. God then makes His own statement about the *Greater Exodus*. As we addressed earlier, God had distinct purposes in the exodus. He wanted Pharaoh, the Egyptians, the Israelites, and the world to know He was the LORD! At the *Greater Exodus*, God re-enforces this point by saying, *"this time I will make them know."* The world is running out of time; God's patience and long-suffering is coming to an end.

Ezekiel is the other prophet who makes a powerful and profound comparison between the exodus and the *Greater Exodus* and succinctly lays out the argument in a prima facie (self-evident) manner.

## COMPARING THE FUTURE WITH THE ANCIENT PAST

> *"As I live," declares the Lord GOD, "surely with a mighty hand and with an outstretched arm and with wrath poured out, I shall be king over you. I will bring you out from the peoples and gather you from the lands where you are scattered, with a mighty hand and with an outstretched arm and with wrath poured out; and I will bring you into the wilderness of the peoples, and there I will enter into judgment with you face to face. As I entered into judgment with your fathers in the wilderness of the land of Egypt, so I will enter into judgment with you," declares the Lord GOD, "I will make you pass under the rod, and I will bring you into the bond of the covenant; and I will purge from you the rebels and those who transgress against Me; I will bring them out of the land where they sojourn, but they will not enter the land of Israel. Thus you will know that I am the LORD."* **Ezekiel 20:33-38**

The language of *"with a mighty hand and with an outstretched arm"* is very much associated with God's role in the exodus story and is often repeated by others.

> *You brought Your people Israel out of the land of Egypt with signs and with wonders, and with a strong hand and with an outstretched arm, and with great terror;*
> **Jeremiah 32:21**

> *Say, therefore, to the sons of Israel, "I am the LORD, and I will bring you out from under the burdens of the Egyptians, and I will deliver you from their bondage. I will also redeem you with an outstretched arm and with great judgments."* **Exodus 6:6**

This expression *"with a strong hand and with an outstretched arm"* then becomes the repeated description throughout the exodus story. When Moses wrote the "repetition of the law"

## COMPARING THE FUTURE WITH THE ANCIENT PAST

(the Book of Deuteronomy), he almost exclusively used this expression to recount the exodus events and to lay out the logic of God's law.

> *You shall remember that you were a slave in the land of Egypt, and the L*ORD *your God brought you out of there by a mighty hand and by an outstretched arm;...*
> **Deuteronomy 5:15a**

> *...the great trials which your eyes saw and the signs and the wonders and the mighty hand and the outstretched arm by which the L*ORD *your God brought you out. So shall the L*ORD *your God do to all the peoples of whom you are afraid.* **Deuteronomy 7:19**

> *Yet they are Your people, even Your inheritance, whom You have brought out by Your great power and Your outstretched arm.* **Deuteronomy 9:29**

> *Know this day that I am not speaking with your sons who have not known and who have not seen the discipline of the L*ORD *your God—His greatness, His mighty hand, and His outstretched arm,* **Deuteronomy 11:2**

> *...and the L*ORD *brought us out of Egypt with a mighty hand and an outstretched arm and with great terror and with signs and wonders;* **Deuteronomy 26:8**

When King Solomon dedicated the temple in Jerusalem, he recounted God's testimony from the exodus and used the same phrase.

> *(for they will hear of Your great name and Your mighty hand, and of Your outstretched arm); when he comes and prays toward this house,...* **1 Kings 8:42**

When it comes to the *Greater Exodus*, we should not be shocked to discover that the same phrase *"with a mighty hand and with an outstretched arm"* is used by Ezekiel to describe the *Greater Exodus*.

Moses, Jeremiah, and others speak to the teaching, but Ezekiel lays out the irrefutable evidence that there will be a future exodus equal to the creation, the redemption, and the second coming. The teaching of the *Greater Exodus* is not an eschatology theory. It is a fundamental teaching of the Scriptures. The leading eschatology teaching among evangelicals is a theory about the timing of the *rapture*. This dominating theory is based on a couple of verses (1 Corinthians 15:51-52 and 1 Thessalonians 4:13-18). In actuality, they are verses describing the resurrection, but it explains how believers who are still alive at the moment are joined with the resurrected assembly. If you step back for a moment and compare the teaching of the rapture with the *Greater Exodus*, a couple of items become obvious.

The emphasis and attention given to the topic of the rapture is completely out of balance with the volume of Scripture about the subject. Two passages of Scripture does **not** make a doctrine; misdirecting the topic to an oblique element is clearly improper, especially when it patently ignores the original topic of the resurrection. But in the case of the *Greater Exodus*, you have already seen how pervasive and specific the Scriptures present the topic. However, the bulk of the Scriptures come from parts of the Bible that most Christians have had very little teaching on nor desire to learn. Tragically, most Christians have a very limited understanding, even about the exodus and even less of the major and minor prophets. Their sense of the future is bound up in a simplistic conclusion or, worse yet, blatant apathy. "No one knows what will happen or when it will happen."

## COMPARING THE FUTURE WITH THE ANCIENT PAST

Nonetheless, the *Greater Exodus* is not an eschatology theory; it is a doctrine as substantive and real as the second coming of the LORD. It sits alongside and is part of the very definition of the God of Abraham, Isaac, and Jacob. It is the Messiah leading the remnant when He returns. Therefore, let us make our faith just as substantive and real by seeking to understand that which God has purposed for us. For us, the story of the exodus is much more than the beginnings of a small nation called Israel.

God accomplished many profound things that are the very foundation of our faith today. These include the definition for redemption, deliverance, and salvation. Add to that the very Word of God came down to the mountain, spoke directly to the people, and gave us the Torah (the first five books of the Scriptures we have today). A tabernacle was built and the glory of the LORD filled it, establishing the standard for how God will be worshipped. As we have said before, there is still more from the ancient story. It is the plan for the future and the last generation.

According to the end-time prophecies, God has planned to add dimension and substance to the topics of salvation and deliverance. Am I suggesting a new salvation or deliverance? Not at all; I am saying that we are going to gain even greater understanding and appreciation for the salvation and deliverance we have already tasted.

Ezekiel's prophecy of a future exodus is directly linked to the exodus with *"As I entered into judgment with your fathers in the wilderness of the land of Egypt, so I will enter into judgment with you," declares the Lord GOD* (Ezekiel 20:36). But how does the *Greater Exodus* go beyond our present understanding of salvation and deliverance? How does God manifest Himself even more than He already has? First, Ezekiel seems to speak of the *Greater Exodus* in more direct and personal terms for every believer, instead of the corporate deliverance of the nation of

Israel. Ezekiel speaks of God's role as the Shepherd in the future exodus with "*I will make you pass under the rod, and I will bring you into the bond of the covenant; and I will purge from you the rebels and those who transgress against Me; I will bring them out of the land where they sojourn, but they will not enter the land of Israel. Thus you will know that I am the LORD.*" (Ezekiel 20:37-38) This is completely consistent with Yeshua referring to Himself as the Great Shepherd.

*Passing under the rod* is a shepherding task. The shepherd's rod serves both as an aid to the sheep and as a weapon against the enemies of the flock. For example, the rod is used as a lever to physically release sheep trapped in a thicket or crevice, to direct a specific sheep, or to wade one's way into the flock. The same rod becomes a blunt weapon to strike or poke against wild animals that would prey on the flock. And finally, the rod serves another important purpose—counting the flock. When a shepherd counts the sheep, they are sequentially passed before the shepherd, and the rod is used to block or permit the sheep to pass in the counting process. The rod can also be used to sort the flock, directing a sheep one way or the other. Ezekiel's use of the expression to *pass under the rod* means that God will personally be involved in the future exodus down to the individual level. He will literally count every one of us.

But there are other reasons why the *Greater Exodus* will deepen our personal relationship with God and unite us as servants of the same king. Let's examine other comparisons.

In the exodus, God poured ten judgments upon Egypt, with the final judgment being the death of the firstborn and then Israel escaped. In the *Greater Exodus*, those who escape will commemorate the first exodus, then depart by faith before the judgments. God's judgments will then fall as twenty-one judgments (3 times 7) with the seven seals, trumpets, and plagues to actually aid in

## COMPARING THE FUTURE WITH THE ANCIENT PAST

their deliverance. In the first exodus, Pharaoh changed his mind about releasing Israel and came to enslave them again. God defended Israel at the Red Sea, delaying Egypt with the cloud. In the *Greater Exodus*, our enemies won't have much time to pursue us. They will be busy with God's judgments perpetually hitting them. Should there be any interface at all (the government is seeking out those who have escaped), they will have to face the cloud and the 144,000.

In the exodus, God used Moses' and Aaron's witness before Pharaoh to announce the judgments coming against Egypt. In the *Greater Exodus*, God has planned for two witnesses to accomplish the same task, announcing His judgments during the great tribulation from the temple mount. But their words will be part of daily news broadcasts worldwide. Pharaoh could dismiss Moses and Aaron as he wished, but the two witnesses won't be shut up. The prophecy says that anyone attempting to stop them or do harm to them will face dire consequences.

> *And if anyone desires to harm them, fire flows out of their mouth and devours their enemies; so if anyone wants to harm them, he must be killed in this way.* **Revelation 11:5**

In the exodus, the judgments which fell on Egypt were directly related to what Egypt believed to be gods. They thought the river Nile, scarabs, the sun, and Pharaoh himself, etc. were gods. The judgments planned for the great tribulation have a similar pattern in that they are judgments upon things which men deem as god-like, including the natural environment, such as trees, the atmosphere, and the waters of rivers, streams, and seas. Some people actually consider Mother Nature to be a god. Environmentalism is an ancient religion masquerading as science today. If you want to find a faith doctrine that is part of the religion of environmentalism, you need not look any further than "global warming." They should be more concerned

97

with the "global warning" that will come from the Messiah when He returns as a consuming fire.

In the exodus, the children of Israel dwelled in mobile shelters using the elements of leafy branches and palms. They traveled in the wilderness for forty years and camped at forty-two different locations. The first camping place of that journey was called "Sukkot," meaning *huts*, *booths*, or *tents*. In the *Greater Exodus*, we will dwell in mobile shelters, having left our homes and cities going into the *wilderness of the peoples*. The first camping place will be called "Sukkot" because we will more than likely camp first where we kept the Feast of Tabernacles also called "Sukkot." It makes sense. It is a place that you know and other like-minded brethren know where to escape initially. Our journey will be 42 months, and we have been promised not to relocate more than 42 times. Yeshua made this promise comparing the number of cities in Israel to the number of future camping locations.

> *...for truly I say to you, you will not finish going through the cities of Israel, until the Son of Man comes.*
> **Matthew 10:23b**

Note: There were 42 cities of Israel with 6 cities of refuge when Yeshua spoke of this limit.

In the exodus, the children of Israel struggled with the issue of adequate food and water. God provided manna and quail for food. He also provided water from a rock. In the *Greater Exodus*, we too will struggle with the issue of adequate food and clean water. God has promised us food, including manna, and has also promised to lead us to springs of water. This truly will be special provision from God because the existing water and food used from the world will become poisonous and part of His judgments.

In the exodus, God provided the children of Israel a cloud by day and a pillar of fire (light) by night. This cloud led them to each of the different campsites. The cloud also stood between the camp and the threats of Pharaoh. The cloud also reflected God's glory and presence in the camp. In the *Greater Exodus* we will be led by the same cloud by day and fire by night, only there will be many of them because of the great number of camps all over the world. The expression *wilderness of the peoples* indicates a multitude of camps and locations.

> *...then the* L*ORD* *will create over the whole area of Mount Zion and over her assemblies a cloud by day, even smoke, and the brightness of a flaming fire by night; for over all the glory will be a canopy. There will be a shelter to give shade from the heat by day, and refuge and protection from the storm and the rain.* **Isaiah 4:5-6**

Isaiah was not referring to the exodus in this passage, he was writing about the remnant of Israel and a future time when the Messianic kingdom would be established. This cloud will not only provide guidance in camp relocation, it will shield us from our enemies. I will explain more about that later, but the cloud will apparently help protect them from the natural elements. This means that the cloud will block harmful radiation from the sun. One of the judgments in the great tribulation is the sun scorching mankind. The cloud may well protect the camp from a storm that includes hail, lightning, and wind storms. Those in the plains of America will need help with tornados.

In the exodus, God Himself defended the children of Israel from the Egyptians, but they had to defend themselves from Amalek (raiders and bandits) along the way. In the same way, we will not be defending ourselves from the governments in the nations through which we journey. God will stand between them and us; however, we will have to defend ourselves from Amalek (bandits, thieves, and savages) that will be in the wilderness setting. There will also be others attempting to escape the government and the judgments hitting the earth. You may be aware of "doomsday preppers" and other survivalists. Some will hunker down and try to hide, but others will become roving bandits, scavenging whatever they can get, attacking the edges of the camp. These are Amalek. With regard to all others in the wilderness setting, they will be hostile in the *Greater Exodus*, attempting to steal food and provisions. We are commanded in the Torah to treat Amalek (meaning those like them) as hostile.

> *...The LORD has sworn; the LORD will have war against Amalek from generation to generation.* **Exodus 17:16**
>
> *Remember what Amalek did to you along the way when you came out from Egypt, how he met you along the way and attacked among you all the stragglers at your rear when you were faint and weary; and he did not fear God. Therefore it shall come about when the LORD your God has given you rest from all your surrounding enemies, in the land which the LORD your God gives you as an inheritance to possess, you will blot out the memory of Amalek from under heaven; you must not forget.* **Deuteronomy 25:17-19**

It is not normal or natural for peace-loving peoples to face warlike conditions. There is a natural tendency to be afraid and avoid hostile conflict at all costs. But in the *Greater Exodus*, this task of defending the camp against *Amalek* will be directed by the 144,000. I will address this item in more detail later. The commandment about Amalek is intended for every generation but especially the final generation in the *Greater Exodus*.

In the exodus, the children of Israel mumbled and grumbled against Moses (the leadership) and God. They even turned away from God, making a god of gold and discussing a return to Egypt.

## COMPARING THE FUTURE WITH THE ANCIENT PAST

There was rebellion in the camp with factions and divisions. Some of them, namely, Korah, Dathan, and Abiram, believed that they could do a better job of leading than Moses and Aaron (Number 16:1-35). In the *Greater Exodus*, there will be mumbling and grumbling as well. There will be rebellion and some will rise up suggesting that they return to their former homes and cities. There will be power struggles, factions, and divisions causing hard feelings. Despite God's warnings and instructions to the contrary, this will probably happen in every camp at some point. The prophecies say that the rebels will be removed, "*and I will purge from you the rebels and those who transgress against Me.*" (Ezekiel 20:38) The Apostle Paul draws from the past mistakes of the exodus and encourages the believers not to make the same mistakes at the end of the ages and the *Greater Exodus*.

> *For I do not want you to be unaware, brethren, that our fathers were all under the cloud and all passed through the sea; and all were baptized into Moses in the cloud and in the sea; and all ate the same spiritual food; and all drank the same spiritual drink, for they were drinking from a spiritual rock which followed them; and the rock was Messiah. Nevertheless, with most of them God was not well-pleased; for they were laid low in the wilderness. Now these things happened as examples for us, that we would not crave evil things, as they also craved. Do not be idolaters, as some of them were; as it is written, "The people sat down to eat and drink, and stood up to play." Nor let us act immorally, as some of them did, and twenty-three thousand fell in one day. Nor let us try the Lord, as some of them did, and were destroyed by the serpents. Nor grumble, as some of them did, and were destroyed by the destroyer. Now these things happened to them as an example, and they were written for our instruction, upon whom the ends of the ages have come. Therefore let him who thinks he stands take heed that he does not fall. No temptation has overtaken you but*

*such as is common to man; and God is faithful, who will not allow you to be tempted beyond what you are able, but with the temptation will provide the way of escape also, that you may be able to endure it.* ***1 Corinthians 10:1-13***

Did you notice that Paul referred to issues in the wilderness as temptations and they would be able to escape and endure? Escaping, surviving, and enduring is the destiny of the tribulation saints in the *Greater Exodus*. In the exodus, only two of the original generation of adults made it from Egypt to the promised land (Joshua and Caleb). In the *Greater Exodus*, the number who make it can't be numbered!

In the exodus, the children of Israel escaped in the dramatic crossing of the Red Sea. God opened the waters and made a dry path of escape while they crossed all through the night. The next morning the waters were allowed to close again, destroying Pharaoh's pursuing chariots.

The prophecy in the Book of Revelation of the believers escaping Judea (Jerusalem area) to the wilderness is similar. Yeshua says that they will flee into the wilderness (the same area where the escaping goat of Yom Kippur is taken) east of Jerusalem just as the great tribulation is beginning (the setting up of the image). However, the dragon (Satan) will use the spring rains to cause a flash flood to endanger their escape. In the *Greater Exodus*, God will open the earth and cause the advancing flood waters to be swallowed up. This is essentially the miracle of the Red Sea in reverse!

In the exodus, the events and methods were limited to one group of people leaving one nation, Egypt. But in the *Greater Exodus*, God will deliver His people from Judea in Israel and every other nation where His people presently dwell. Salvation and deliverance will be worldwide. There won't be just one pillar or just one camp. There will be many camps in many locations as God brings us out of the remotest parts, *the ends of the earth*.

We don't yet know exactly how all of this will work. For example, one of the intriguing questions that will be answered in those days concerns the multiple campsites and differing wildernesses. Will these groups cluster together and become larger assemblies (tens of thousands and hundreds of thousands) as a result of meeting each other? Or, will God keep them distributed in smaller camps of hundreds and thousands? In the exodus, we estimate that the camp with the twelve tribes and the Levites was between two and three million souls. Maybe the future exodus will become a huge assembly in every nation or continental area. Whatever happens, it will be a *Greater Exodus*.

# COMPARING THE FUTURE WITH THE ANCIENT PAST

TEN

# HOW JUDAISM PREPARES FOR THE GREATER EXODUS

Passover is recognized as the Jewish festival of freedom, commemorating the redemption of the children of Israel from Egyptian bondage. In Jewish observance today, Passover (Pesach) is actually a meld of several biblical holidays, although Scripture gives them each their own recognition. First, the Passover itself is observed by holding a Passover seder (order) dinner. Because unleavened bread (matzah) is eaten during the seder, the day is combined with the seven day festival of *Unleavened Bread*. In the midst of these eight days, the *Feast of First Fruits* also occurs depending on when the first regular sabbath day falls. It is from First Fruits that the counting of the omer (fifty days) is started, leading to the *Feast of Weeks* (Shavuot). An omer is a unit of measure for grain. It is also the counting method for the seven Sabbaths and the fifty days.

The combination of Passover and Unleavened Bread, which commemorates the exodus of Egypt, reminds Israel of the final judgment (the death of the firstborn in Egypt) and eating the bread of haste as they escaped from Pharaoh. However, Passover observance is not just an annual commemoration about the past. Much of the observance of Passover for observant Jews is about the future. For generations the final words of the Passover seder were "Next year in Jerusalem!" Until the modern state of

Israel was established, Passover was the single moment in the year when Jews worldwide looked to a better future. *Next year in Jerusalem* is the rallying cry of the "final redemption."

When the Jews refer to the *final redemption*, they are referring to a future exodus, an exodus that will bring all of the scattered of Israel back to the promised land. Traditional Jewish theology ranging from Reform to Orthodox believes in this future *Greater Exodus* and has done so for many centuries.

As with every Sabbath and God's appointed times, a certain amount of preparation is required to successfully enjoy the event. Every weekly Sabbath has a day of preparation (Friday) and the seven feasts require additional preparatory activities. In the case of Passover, a significant effort is made to remove all leaven from the house. It is a little bit comical to watch an observant Jewish Deli owner or a baker dispose of their "leaven" while observing the eight days of Pesach. There are stories of owners selling their shops to a Gentile for $1 and then purchasing it back after the feast day is complete. But removal of leaven for the Passover is not the only preparation. Traditional Judaism offers special spiritual preparation in their weekly teachings leading up to the observance of Passover. In fact, there are three special Sabbaths with specific Haftorah (after the Torah) teachings given in addition to the normal weekly teachings sequencing through the Torah cycle. It is from these additional preparatory teachings that specific customs have been embedded in the Passover Seder and the stage is set to shout "Next year in Jerusalem!"

## SHABBAT PARAH

This special Sabbath follows the observance of Purim (the Feast of Lots) about a month before Passover and is the first of the three special Haftorah teachings to prepare the Jews to keep the

Passover. Parah is about the "red heifer" whose ashes are used in the waters of purification. The teaching comes from Ezekiel 36:16-38. Parah also means "fruitful" and this passage promises a future time when Israel will flourish and be fruitful. This does **not** appear to be a review of the exodus from Egypt. Instead, the prophet is explaining why Israel has been scattered to the nations and about a future gathering from exile.

> *Then the word of the LORD came to me saying, Son of man, when the house of Israel was living in their own land, they defiled it by their ways and their deeds; their way before Me was like the uncleanness of a woman in her impurity. Therefore I poured out My wrath on them for the blood which they had shed on the land, because they had defiled it with their idols. Also I scattered them among the nations, and they were dispersed throughout the lands. According to their ways and their deeds I judged them. When they came to the nations where they went, they profaned My holy name, because it was said of them, "These are the people of the LORD; yet they have come out of His land." But I had concern for My holy name, which the house of Israel had profaned among the nations where they went.*
> **Ezekiel 36:16-21**

Despite this traditional teaching, I'm not sure that my Jewish brethren have ever really accepted God's justification for exiling them to the nations. Israel's tendency, which is true of all peoples, has been to rationalize and make excuses for why they find themselves in a time of judgment. In this generation, we have grown accustomed to our homes in exile, and the last thing we want to hear is that we bear any responsibility for being exiled. "That happened to our ancestors, not us," is the common excuse.

The prophet Jeremiah takes up this same subject as Ezekiel. Jeremiah speaks into the future to our present day generation citing our responsibilities in this matter and explaining why we are still in exile. Jeremiah makes a comparison of our own sins with those of our fathers before and concludes that our sins in the nations now are worse than the ones that got our ancestors exiled to begin with.

> *Now when you tell this people all these words that they will say to you, "For what reason has the LORD declared all this great calamity against us? And what is our iniquity, or what is our sin which we have committed against the LORD our God?" Then you are to say to them, "It is because your forefathers have forsaken Me," declares the LORD, "and have followed other gods and served them and bowed down to them; but Me they have forsaken and have not kept My law. You too have done evil, even more than your forefathers; for behold, you are each one walking according to the stubbornness of his own evil heart, without listening to Me. So I will hurl you out of this land into the land which you have not known, neither you nor your fathers; and there you will serve other gods day and night, for I will grant you no favor."* **Jeremiah 16:10-13**

It is fascinating that the first preparatory subject for the Passover each year is to understand why Israel is in exile and the adjoining responsibilities in that matter. The preparatory instruction continues. Look at what Jeremiah says immediately after reminding Israel of their sins and judgment of exile.

> *"Therefore behold, days are coming," declares the LORD, "when it will no longer be said, 'As the LORD lives, who brought up the sons of Israel out of the land of Egypt,' but, 'As the LORD lives, who brought up the sons of Israel from the land of the north and from all the countries where He had banished them.' For I will restore them to their own land which I gave to their fathers."* **Jeremiah 16:14-15**

## HOW JUDAISM PREPARES FOR THE GREATER EXODUS

It is one of the foundational Scriptures defining the *Greater Exodus*. Compare this with Ezekiel's words about the *Greater Exodus* and God's reasons for bringing us back.

*Therefore, say to the house of Israel, 'Thus says the Lord GOD, "It is not for your sake, O house of Israel, that I am about to act, but for My holy name, which you have profaned among the nations where you went. I will vindicate the holiness of My great name which has been profaned among the nations, which you have profaned in their midst. Then the nations will know that I am the LORD," declares the Lord GOD, "when I prove Myself holy among you in their sight. For I will take you from the nations, gather you from all the lands, and bring you into your own land. Then I will sprinkle clean water on you, and you will be clean; I will cleanse you from all your filthiness and from all your idols. Moreover, I will give you a new heart and put a new spirit within you; and I will remove the heart of stone from your flesh and give you a heart of flesh. I will put My Spirit within you and cause you to walk in My statutes, and you will be careful to observe My ordinances. You will live in the land that I gave to your forefathers; so you will be My people, and I will be your God. Moreover, I will save you from all your uncleanness; and I will call for the grain and multiply it, and I will not bring a famine on you. I will multiply the fruit of the tree and the produce of the field, so that you will not receive again the disgrace of famine among the nations. Then you will remember your evil ways and your deeds that were not good, and you will loathe yourselves in your own sight for your iniquities and your abominations. I am not doing this for your sake," declares the Lord GOD, "let it be known to you. Be ashamed and confounded for your ways, O house of Israel!"*

**Ezekiel 36:22-32**

Ezekiel speaks of being cleansed as instructed in Shabbat Parah. This is a preparatory act with the ashes of the red heifer used in the waters of purification. Both Jeremiah and Ezekiel tell the same message of exile followed by the promise of the *Greater Exodus*. Dr. J. H. Hertz, the former Chief Rabbi of the British Empire, offers his commentary on this special Haftorah teaching in his one-volume Chumash entitled *The Pentateuch and Haftorahs* (Second Edition, Soncino Press, London, 1985, pg 999). He succinctly defines the future return of the exiles needing purification and a repentant heart before the "final redemption"—the *Greater Exodus*.

"The Additional Reading lays down the regulations for bodily purification. The object of these laws, our Sages say, was to impress on the Israelites the need of moral purification after the apostasy in connection with the Golden Calf."

"Moral purification is likewise the theme of the Haftorah taken from the Book of Ezekiel. How Israel is to emerge from the grave of the Exile, renew its life on its own soil, and open an era of undefiled service of God—such is the teaching of the Haftorah. God had justly sent Israel into captivity, says the Prophet; its disasters were inevitable, seeing that God is a God of Holiness and Right. But the heathens had misunderstood this punishment, taking it as a sign of God's inability to save His people (Rashi, Kimchi). In this way, Israel had occasioned the profanation of God's Name. To vindicate His own honour, God will restore them; not because Israel deserved restoration, but because God's Glory demanded it. This Restoration will, however, be accompanied, by moral renewal; on the one hand, God will implant 'a new heart and a new spirit' in the nation; and, on the other hand, Israel's soul will be swept by sincere Repentance that will cause it to be

## HOW JUDAISM PREPARES FOR THE GREATER EXODUS

ashamed of its evil past. When the sinful nation has thus been purified, and the desolate land re-peopled, then the heathen will know the whole is God's doing."

So, what is the underlying truth in this message of returning from exile and why is it preparatory to Passover each year? There is a future Passover that will initiate the final redemption, the restoration, and the *Greater Exodus*. Each new Passover could be the one. Therefore, Israel prepares their hearts each year for what they will do in the future exodus.

## SHABBAT HACHODESH

Shabbat HaChodesh is the second preparatory Haftorah leading to Passover. It is the Sabbath at the beginning of the month of Nisan (Aviv), the month in which Passover takes place. Again, the Haftorah of Shabbat HaChodesh is again **not** about ancient Egypt and the exodus. The reading is taken from Ezekiel 45:16-46:18. This passage is a description of the first Passover ***to be observed in the Messianic kingdom*** when the Prince (Messiah) will lead the temple ceremony.

> *In the first month, on the fourteenth day of the month* [in the kingdom], *you shall have the Passover, a feast of seven days; unleavened bread shall be eaten. On that day the prince* [the Messiah] *shall provide for himself and all the people of the land a bull for a sin offering. During the seven days of the feast he shall provide as a burnt offering to the* LORD *seven bulls and seven rams without blemish on every day of the seven days, and a male goat daily for a sin offering. He shall provide as a grain offering an ephah with a bull, an ephah with a ram and a hin of oil with an ephah.* **Ezekiel 45:21-24**

Every one of us, in preparing for the future Passover that leads to the great tribulation and the *Greater Exodus*, should view ourselves all the way to the kingdom with the Messiah. The Passovers of the future will be significant. The Passover that starts the *Greater Exodus* will be very important, but the first Passover in the kingdom led by the Prince (Messiah) will be extremely important to us. Yeshua referred to the Passover in the kingdom when He refused to drink the last cup (the Cup of Praise) with the disciples, saying that He would not drink of it until in the kingdom. Yeshua therefore offered His own commentary about this Haftorah and the future Passover described by Ezekiel that He would lead in the kingdom.

> *"But I say to you, I will not drink of this fruit of the vine from now on until that day when I drink it new with you in My Father's kingdom."* **Matthew 26:29**

## SHABBAT HAGADOL

Shabbat Hagadol is the third preparatory Haftorah teaching which precedes Passover. Shabbat Hagadol means "The Great Sabbath" (the weekly Sabbath just prior to Passover).

The reading for the Haftorah is taken from Malachi 3:4 through 4:4. Like the Shabbat Parah, this reading concerns Israel's disobedience in the nations, but it concludes with a prophecy about Elijah coming before the *day of the* Lord.

A special cup, *the cup of Elijah*, is set on the Passover table and is treated separately from the four traditional cups of the seder. After the third and before the fourth traditional cup is drunk, the cup of Elijah is filled to the brim as an enticement to get Elijah to join the Passover seder prior to its conclusion. Once the cup is poured, children are sent to the door of the house to call Elijah into the house. Why are they looking for Elijah at Passover? The answer is part of the instruction of the Haftorah. If Elijah joins the Passover, then everyone will know they are at the end of the

## HOW JUDAISM PREPARES FOR THE GREATER EXODUS

ages, and the exile of the nations is finished—that that Passover is the one to escape for the *Greater Exodus*.

I have kept many Passover seders and Elijah has never been at my door yet, but the anticipation grows with each year. From this Haftorah teaching, Israel is instructed to anticipate Elijah. They understand that his appearance specifically signifies *that* Passover seder as the beginning of the *Greater Exodus*! How will this be fulfilled? Will Elijah come and join everyone's seder like Santa Claus visits every house on Christmas eve? Of course not. This will probably find its fulfillment at the same time the two witnesses appear on the temple mount after the Abomination of Desolation, just prior to Passover. Many believe that one of the two witnesses may be Elijah or someone "in the spirit of Elijah." Therefore, when the two witnesses appear, the seder that follows will already have the spirit of Elijah at their seder. The Tribulation Timeline (Appendix A) shows a Passover immediately after the Abomination of Desolation and the two witnesses appearing in Jerusalem. This is the Passover that will be the cue for the remnant of Israel to escape their homes and cities and proceed into the *wilderness of the peoples*.

> *Remember the law of Moses My servant, even the statutes and ordinances which I commanded him in Horeb for all Israel. Behold, I am going to send you Elijah the prophet before the coming of the great and terrible day of the LORD. He will restore the hearts of the fathers to their children, and the hearts of the children to their fathers, so that I will not come and smite the land with a curse.*
> **Malachi 4:4-6**

There is much commentary about restoring the *hearts of the fathers to their children, and the hearts of the children to their fathers*. Foremost in the commentary is the key word "restore." The *Greater Exodus* is about restoration, restoring Israel to their

Heavenly Father, and being restored to the land. But the expressions *fathers to their children* and *children to their fathers* is specifically noted. It is neither redundant nor superlative. The proper interpretation is found in determining which "fathers" are being referred to. For example, are the fathers Abraham, Isaac, and Jacob those "fathers"? To some extent, you would have to say "yes," but there may be more to this when you consider the *Greater Exodus*. What about our fathers who came out of Egypt and all who have lived leading up to the final generation? Isn't the *Greater Exodus* about restoration and being gathered together in the kingdom? Moses offers something very special about fathers and sons, part of the Parashat (the Torah portion) Nitzavim teaching, just before he explained the *Greater Exodus* in Deuteronomy 30. The following verse is the last verse of chapter 29 which leads to the words of chapter 30.

> *The secret things belong to the* LORD *our God, but the things revealed belong to us and to our sons forever, that we may observe all the words of this law.*
> **Deuteronomy 29:29**

The sages of Israel (the previous teachers of Judaism) say that the expression *to our sons forever* is referring to the final generation of mortals before we step into the immortality of the Messianic kingdom. Moses is talking about the actual fathers who came out of Egypt and their future sons who will be part of the *Greater Exodus*. Elijah's work of restoring fathers to children and children to fathers stretches from the exodus to the *Greater Exodus*! Therefore, this preparatory Sabbath (Shabbat Hagadol) and its reading from Malachi is a final reminder of our fathers who were part of the exodus. When we see ourselves as their sons, we link the exodus to the *Greater Exodus*.

Now here is something even more intriguing about verse 29. The ancient Scribes placed "jots" (dots) above each letter in the phrase "to our sons forever." These Scribal marks are copied in every Sefer Torah scroll and are considered to be part of the Word of God. This is highly significant, requiring the Torah teacher to consider a deeper teaching of the passage. There are three other places in the Torah where these "jots" are placed. As a result, there is a linked teaching of all four places. These four locations link four topics:

1. The conflict of Esau and Jacob
2. The story of Jacob sending Joseph
3. The redemption of the firstborn and
4. The future sons of the *Greater Exodus*.

This Scribal teaching is similar to the homiletic teaching in Isaiah called the "Consolation of Israel, the Redemption of Jerusalem." This is a Scribal teaching of "what happens to the fathers will happen to the sons." It is drawing the prophetic teaching out of the past. What is being said? Answer: There will be a great conflict that originates with Esau and Jacob (the present Middle East conflict and the world today) that will be the setting for the final redemption. The firstborn of Israel (the remnant of Israel) will be counted and gathered. The final generation of sons will be part of the *Greater Exodus* to the true promised land.

In the Passover seder, the story of Joseph being sent by Jacob to see to the welfare of the flock and his brothers is the beginning of the story of redemption in Scripture. The sages link the ancient story to the future, calling it the "final redemption." The teaching of the final redemption leads you to the other prophecies referring to the restoration of the whole house of Jacob. By the way, the first verses of the story of redemption are Genesis 37:12-13.

*Then his brothers went to pasture their father's flock in Shechem. Israel said to Joseph, "Are not your brothers*

*pasturing the flock in Shechem? Come, and I will send you to them." And he said to him, "I will go."*
**Genesis 37:12 -13**

There is another unique twist in the Scriptures with the translation of verse 12. Some translators say "Jacob's" flock instead of "their father's" flock. In actuality, neither translation is literal. In the Hebrew, two letters, the Aleph and Tav, form the word "et" in the text. The Aleph Tav is another teaching about the Messiah. The Messiah said of Himself, He is the Aleph and Tav (Christians say Alpha and Omega) but He really was the Hebrew Messiah. The Aleph Tav flock is the Messiah's flock and He is the Great Shepherd. This affirms to those who believe in His redemption that these verses really are the beginning of the story of redemption. The redemption story is the story of a father who sends his son, who is rejected by his own brothers, cast in a pit, who comes out of the pit, and later is ruler of the world (the story of Joseph). It is also the story of the Messiah (the story of redemption). One statement that Yeshua often used would infuriate the religious leaders of His day. It was the simple words, "My Father sent Me" or "I was sent by the Father." Yeshua was directly referencing Genesis 37:13 and they knew it.

There are other traditional teachings and readings as a part of the Jewish observance of Pesach (Passover). They include the first and second days of Passover. They too have special readings, along with the weekly Sabbath that falls during the Feast of Unleavened Bread, and then on the final day of the Pesach. The final special teaching is a supplemental reading from the prophet Isaiah 10:32-12:6. It begins with the topic of the Messiah and how He is anointed with the seven spirits of God (the Spirit of the LORD, wisdom, understanding, counsel, strength, knowledge, and the fear of the LORD). Because He has those seven Spirits, He will have the authority to rule the coming Messianic kingdom. It goes on to define the Messianic kingdom where the wolf lies down with the lamb, the calf with the lion, etc. Then the message shifts into a final thought. It is again the subject of the *Greater Exodus* that leads to the kingdom.

> *¹¹Then it will happen on that day that the* L ORD *will again recover the second time with His hand the remnant of His people, who will remain, from Assyria, Egypt, Pathros, Cush, Elam, Shinar, Hamath, and from the islands of the sea. ¹²And He will lift up a standard for the nations, and assemble the banished ones of Israel, and will gather the dispersed of Judah from the four corners of the earth. ¹³Then the jealousy of Ephraim will depart, and those who harass Judah will be cut off; Ephraim will not be jealous of Judah, and Judah will not harass Ephraim… ¹⁶And there will be a highway from Assyria for the remnant of His people who will be left, just as there was for Israel in the day that they came up out of the land of Egypt.* **Isaiah 11:11-13, 16**

There is going to be a second exodus *just as there was for Israel in the day that they came up out of the land of Egypt*. Rabbi Hertz offers his commentary for this specific teaching on page 1023.

> "Intimately bound up with the Jewish Messianic hope is the thought of the Passover of the future. It will be a new redemption and a new Exodus, this time an exodus of the Jewish people from the lands of their dispersion and an ingathering into the Holy Land."
> **The Pentateuch and Haftorahs**
> (Second Edition, Soncino Press, London, 1985)

Rabbi Hertz fails to understand that it will be more than just the Jewish people, but he does understand there will be a new Exodus. Many Jewish teachers summarize the preparation for Passover and the future Passover of the *Greater Exodus* this way. While the first night of Passover commemorates the redemption from exile in Egypt, the final day of the Feast of Unleavened Bread celebrates the future redemption, which God will bring about through the Messiah. The traditional Jewish observance of Passover actually promotes preparation for the *Greater Exodus*. I believe they are correct in their promotion, but like Moses said they still don't see nor hear all that God is doing. They will be surprised when Yeshua leads the Passover in the kingdom. It will be a little bit like when Joseph revealed himself to his brethren as the Viceroy of Egypt. They will be speechless with their mouths open. Actually, I think all of the believers will experience some of that.

ELEVEN

# HOW MESSIANICS PREPARE FOR THE GREATER EXODUS

First, let us define the term "Messianics." Christians are named Christians based on the Greek word "Christos" for Christ. Messianics are named Messianics based on the Hebrew word "Meshiach" for Messiah. Messianics emphasize the Hebraic definitions and understandings as compared with Christians. Even further, there are many Messianic Jews (Jews who believe that Yeshua of Nazareth is the Messiah). But not everyone is a Messianic Jew who uses that term. Many, and in fact, most of the believers in the Messianic Movement of this generation are former Christians who have chosen to keep the commandments, particularly Sabbath, biblical kosher, and the Appointed Times (Feasts of the Lord). They congregate in Messianic congregations and assemblies. They have turned away from basic Christian culture including Christmas and Easter. Messianics, therefore, are believers of Yeshua seeking to assemble and observe the biblical commandments. At a spiritual level, they identify with the remnant of Israel and the children of promise. At a natural level, some may be native born (descending from one of the tribes of Israel) or they may be from the nations (believing aliens and sojourners). They all believe in the God of Israel and proclaim Him to be the One, True God. One of the Appointed Times they observe is the Feast of Ingathering.

The Feast of Ingathering is also called the Feast of Tabernacles or the Feast of Booths. In the Hebrew language it is called *Sukkot*. A single shelter is called a *sukkah*. It is interesting to note that the first camping place of the children of Israel upon leaving Egypt was called *Succoth*. It is the seventh feast of the LORD defined in Leviticus 23.

> *On exactly the fifteenth day of the seventh month, when you have gathered in the crops of the land, you shall celebrate the feast of the LORD for seven days, with a rest on the first day and a rest on the eighth day. Now on the first day you shall take for yourselves the foliage of beautiful trees, palm branches and boughs of leafy trees and willows of the brook; and you shall rejoice before the LORD your God for seven days. You shall thus celebrate it as a feast to the LORD for seven days in the year. It shall be a perpetual statute throughout your generations; you shall celebrate it in the seventh month. You shall live in booths for seven days; all the native-born in Israel shall live in booths, so that your generations may know that I had the sons of Israel live in booths when I brought them out from the land of Egypt. I am the LORD your God.* **Leviticus 23:39-43**

The seventh month of the Hebrew calendar is called Tishrei. This is also referred to as the "turn of the year" in the fall after the harvest. Tishrei actually has three holy day periods. On 1 Tishrei is Yom Teruah (day of the Trumpets), also call Rosh Hashanah (Jewish New Year). Then on 10 Tishrei is Yom Kippur (Day of Atonement). This day is considered to be one of the most holy, if not the most holy, and solemn day in the annual cycle. Five days later, the Feast of Tabernacles is observed for seven days; then on the eighth day of Tabernacles is the "Great Day of the Feast" making the Feast a total of eight days (Leviticus 23: 34-36). The first and eighth days of the feast are also called "High Sabbaths."

## HOW MESSIANICS PREPARE FOR THE GREATER EXODUS

The actual title of "Ingathering" seems logical as the Torah speaks of the timing of the holy days associated with the harvest. For example, the wheat harvest is completed in the late spring/early summer, the same season as the Feast of Weeks. The final harvest of fruit is completed in late summer and early fall, the same season as the Feast of Ingathering.

*Also you shall observe the Feast of the Harvest of the first fruits of your labors from what you sow in the field; also the Feast of the Ingathering at the end of the year when you gather in the fruit of your labors from the field.*
**Exodus 23:16**

Later, after the temple was built in Jerusalem, pilgrims would travel and set up their sukkot (temporary shelters) to be part of the festival in the Jerusalem area. Many sacrifices were presented, and four great lights were set up in the temple to replicate the cloud by day and fire by night that led their ancestors through the wilderness to the land. The feast had a two-fold objective: (1) remember how their ancestors lived (in sukkot) when they traveled from Egypt to the promised land and (2) to rejoice before the Lord. We often refer to this feast today as the "season of our joy." We are not jumping around crushing grapes to make wine at the end of the harvest like an agricultural holiday. The joy of our feast is directed toward worship in anticipation of the future kingdom.

Many Messianic brethren today observe the feast by actually "camping out" with other brethren in their temporary shelters for the entire eight days. While they cannot perform all of the elements of the feast because of the lack of a temple and priests in Jerusalem, they keep the commandment with their hearts even though they are still scattered in the nations. As a result, they literally have a bonding experience with their own families and within the community of faith in preparation for the *Greater Exodus*.

## HOW MESSIANICS PREPARE FOR THE GREATER EXODUS

Some evangelical Christians also keep the Feast of Tabernacles in a unique way. The International Christian Embassy has for many years hosted a conference in Jerusalem during the Feast of Tabernacles. It is more of a "pro-Israel rally" than a remembrance of the Egyptian exodus. They don't stay in sukkot, unless you consider a hotel as one, but it is an excellent effort on the part of many believers around the world to remember the holy days and draw attention to the miracle of modern Israel. I mention these two types of observance, because they force the participants to get up out of their houses and live in temporary housing. This is a key element in keeping the Feast. It is a reminder of the exodus living in temporary but mobile housing.

In addition to the actual observance, there is a prophetic aspect to the feast that concerns the end of the ages. The traditional observance of Sukkot involves leafy branches such as myrtle or palm. These are excellent materials for the roof of a traditional sukkah. The tribulation saints in Revelation 7:9 are seen holding palm branches (as specified in Leviticus 23:39-43). These palm branches indicate that the tribulation saints are prepared to observe Sukkot. It is believed that this will be the first event of the kingdom for the saints with the Messiah, based on the prophetic sequence of the fall holidays.

The Feast of Trumpets (Yom Teruah) will signal the resurrection and gathering of all saints, the Day of Atonement (Yom Kippur) signifies the *day of the* LORD (God's judgment), and then the Feast of Tabernacles (Sukkot) follows. It is prophesied that at the conclusion of the *Greater Exodus* and the beginning of the Messianic kingdom the saints will all be gathered to observe the Feast of Ingathering! That definitely will be a season of joy!

*Then it will come about that any who are left of all the nations that went against Jerusalem will go up from year to year to worship the King, the* LORD *of hosts, and to celebrate the Feast of Booths.* **Zechariah 14:16**

Those who are "left of all the nations" is referring to the remnant of Israel that is brought out of those nations. All of the nations will have joined with the antimessiah at the end to fight against the Messiah by fighting Jerusalem, but in the end Jerusalem will become a place of joy when the LORD returns and the remnant celebrates the Feast of Booths!

The Prophet Amos also speaks of the Feast of Tabernacles at the beginning of the Messianic Kingdom following the *day of the* LORD, when we will begin the process of rebuilding and having a part in the Messianic age and kingdom.

> *[11] "In that day I will raise up the fallen booth of David, and wall up its breaches; I will also raise up its ruins, and rebuild it as in the days of old;" [13] "Behold, days are coming," declares the* LORD, *"When the plowman will overtake the reaper and the treader of grapes him who sows seed; when the mountains will drip sweet wine and all the hills will be dissolved. [14] Also I will restore the captivity of My people Israel, and they will rebuild the ruined cities and live in them; they will also plant vineyards and drink their wine, and make gardens and eat their fruit. [15] I will also plant them on their land, and they will not again be rooted out from their land which I have given them," Says the* LORD *your God.* **Amos 9:11, 13-15**

Did you notice the word "booth" (*sukkah* in Jewish bibles) at the beginning of the passage? It is referring to the mobile shelter used during a Feast of Tabernacles. Many Bible commentators make the simple mistake of thinking that this is the "tabernacle of David" and is referring to the temple in Jerusalem. Many translations use the word "tabernacle" and this leads some readers to think of the temple in Jerusalem. But the truth is, the "tabernacle" is referring to a sukkah, not the temple. This passage is quoted by James in Acts 15:16-18 as part of the justification for the nations (Gentiles) coming to the faith. James referenced the passage to justify that the aliens and sojourners who believe in the Messiah are expected to part of the *Greater Exodus* and should be welcomed by the native born into the faith of the God of Israel and His Messiah.

This is not the only reference from the prophets used in the New Testament. The Apostle Paul quotes both Hosea and Isaiah declaring that many from the nations (former Gentiles) will be part of the *Greater Exodus*.

> *Yet the number of the sons of Israel will be like the sand of the sea, which cannot be measured or numbered; and in the place where it is said to them, "You are not My people," it will be said to them, "You are the sons of the living God." And the sons of Judah and the sons of Israel will be gathered together, and they will appoint for themselves one leader, and they will go up from the land, for great will be the day of Jezreel.* **Hosea 1:10-11**

Paul quotes this passage in Romans chapter 9 as part of his justification to be the Apostle to the Gentiles (nations); however, the exegesis of this passage is clearly about the House of Israel (the Northern kingdom). It literally explains that the House of Israel will be gathered back to Israel again after their exile. It also says that the Messiah will be their one leader and that they will be joined with the House of Judah. It is also describing a *Greater Exodus* back to the land after the *day of the* L ORD. Paul understood this prophecy to be a part of our New Covenant faith. He used the authority of this prophecy to justify his own ministry reaching out to the Gentiles.

## HOW MESSIANICS PREPARE FOR THE GREATER EXODUS

Moses prophetically saw what would happen to Israel after they crossed the Jordan. He knew they would be scattered to the nations. However, he didn't see this as dismissing the covenant God made with Israel or as the end of the people of Israel. He saw the God of Israel remaining faithful and one day bringing the exiles back to the land, just as God had led them out of Egypt earlier.

It almost seems that Moses knew there would be someone arguing in a future day that God had rejected Israel, scattered them throughout the world, and rejected the covenant He made with Israel. His answer refutes the main argument of *replacement theology* we hear today.

> *Yet if in spite of this you* [Israel] *do not obey Me, but act with hostility against Me* [rejecting the Messiah], *then I will act with wrathful hostility against you; and I, even I, will punish you seven times for your sins. Further, you will eat the flesh of your sons and the flesh of your daughters you will eat. I then will destroy your high places, and cut down your incense altars, and heap your remains on the remains of your idols, for My soul shall abhor you. I will lay waste your cities as well and will make your sanctuaries desolate, and I will not smell your soothing aromas. I will make the land desolate so that your enemies who settle in it will be appalled over it. You, however, I will scatter among the nations and will draw out a sword after you, as your land becomes desolate and your cities become waste. Then the land will enjoy its sabbaths all the days of the desolation, while you are in your enemies' land; then the land will rest and enjoy its sabbaths. All the days of its desolation it will observe the rest which it did not observe on your sabbaths, while you were living on it. As for those of you who may be left, I will also bring weakness into their hearts in the lands of their enemies. And the sound*

*of a driven leaf will chase them, and even when no one is pursuing they will flee as though from the sword, and they will fall. They will therefore stumble over each other as if running from the sword, although no one is pursuing; and you will have no strength to stand up before your enemies. But you will perish among the nations, and your enemies' land will consume you. So those of you who may be left will rot away because of their iniquity in the lands of your enemies; and also because of the iniquities of their forefathers they will rot away with them.* **Leviticus 26:27-39**

All of this has happened and we can see the truth of Moses' words in history. Remember, Moses prophesied 3500 years into the future (the present day) when he spoke of God bringing the scattered of Israel (and anyone else who believes in Him) back to the promised land.

*If they* [Israel] *confess their iniquity and the iniquity of their forefathers, in their unfaithfulness which they committed against Me, and also in their acting with hostility against Me—I also was acting with hostility against them, to bring them into the land of their enemies—or if their uncircumcised heart becomes humbled so that they then make amends for their iniquity, then I will remember My covenant with Jacob, and I will remember also My covenant with Isaac, and My covenant with Abraham as well, and I will remember the land. For the land will be abandoned by them, and will make up for its sabbaths while it is made desolate without them. They, meanwhile, will be making amends for their iniquity, because they rejected My ordinances and their soul abhorred My statutes. Yet in spite of this, when they are in the land of their enemies, I will not reject them, nor will I so abhor them as to destroy them, breaking My covenant with them; for I am the* LORD *their God. But I will remember for them the covenant with their ancestors, whom I brought out of the land of Egypt in the sight of the nations, that I might be their God. I am the* LORD. **Leviticus 26:40-45**

Many Christian teachers do not seem to understand the breadth of the covenant that God made with Israel, and they do not understand how God Himself remembers and maintains the covenant for the sake of the fathers despite the misdeeds of their descendants. Even Jews misunderstand what Moses really taught, what the Messiah was doing when He came the first time, and the teaching of the Apostles.

God pledged to keep both parts of Abraham's covenant and the covenant made with Moses for Israel. God has pledged that He will **not** reject Israel, or so abhor her as to destroy her, nor break the covenant made with her. Instead, He has said that He will remember it for His people. This is why the Messiah was willing and had to die for us. He was keeping *our* part of the covenant (the part we failed to keep) with our father Abraham and with Moses. The people of Israel, and we who believe in the Messiah today, are the descendants of Abraham, not because of our physical birth or by our own will. We are Abraham's descendants by the grace of God and faith in His promises. The *Greater Exodus* is the destiny of the descendants of Abraham, those who by faith hold to the promise of God and His sacrifice of Yeshua. His sacrifice serves as our payment for failing to keep God's covenant and justice demanded by God's law.

This is part of the reason why God has given us festivals to memorialize (remember) what the LORD has done. With every memorial comes a reminder of what God has done and a prophetic picture for us at the end of the ages.

Had you and I lived together 2,000 years ago waiting for the Messiah to appear, and you wanted to understand what the

Messiah would do, I would have recommended that you focus on the Passover, the Feast of Unleavened Bread, and the Feast of First Fruits. These tell the story and symbolize the redemptive work that the Messiah would do. Now, some 2,000 years later, we all desire to know the end-time events and what the Messiah will be doing. It is almost the same recommendation, but you should learn all you can about the fall feast of Trumpets, the Day of Atonement, and the Feast of Tabernacles to understand how the Messiah will accomplish the work of Restoration. Embedded in the Feast of Tabernacles is the escape plan of the *Greater Exodus*. Still further, the first Feast of Tabernacles in the kingdom will be the final conclusion for the *Greater Exodus*.

Just as you must get up out of your house, gather your sukkah (mobile shelter) and some other items to camp, you have actually done the same preparatory steps to begin the *Greater Exodus*. You are actually practicing to escape, survive, and endure with your sukkah.

Keeping the Feast of Tabernacles is more than just family camping fun. You must prepare for the environment, including hot/cold, wet/dry, windy/calm, humidity, bugs, sunburn, smoke, and animals at night. You must plan for a host of activities, including shelter set-up, meal preparation and eating, bathing, building camp fires, keeping kids happy and safe, keeping "Mama" warm and dry. You then come to worship the LORD and join with others in singing, dancing, fellowshipping, and learning. In some respects it is just like going through the great tribulation! (In fact, I share with my fellow campers that if you do not keep Mama warm and dry while at the feast, then you will suffer great tribulation.)

That is what the lesson of the Feast of Tabernacles is supposed to teach. We are to remember and learn how God preserved our

# HOW MESSIANICS PREPARE FOR THE GREATER EXODUS

ancestors in the wilderness after leaving Egypt. Each year at the completion of eight days of Tabernacles (thoroughly exhausted), I confess that I have no idea how Moses did this for forty years in the wilderness, but this is what we are supposed to learn. They only made it because God delivered them. We will only make it in the *Greater Exodus* by God's grace as well.

The Feast of Tabernacles trains you and your whole family for the future *Greater Exodus*. When people ask me where we will escape to first at the start of the *Greater Exodus*, I tell them where they last kept the Feast of Tabernacles. That place is called "Sukkot." The first place the children of Israel escaped to when leaving Egypt was called "Sukkot." That is where they first set up their mobile shelters. I believe it will be the first camping place in the great tribulation. It is how the *Greater Exodus* begins as well. For those of you who don't keep the Feast of Tabernacles, you are denying yourself critical training for the *Greater Exodus*. I would heartily recommend that you join like-minded brethren and keep the Appointed Times of the Lord.

Having experienced the "joy" and the "tribulation practice" of the Feast of Tabernacles, I have concluded that physical preparation for observing the Feast of Tabernacles is directly proportional to the preparation for the *Greater Exodus* and the great tribulation. That is, bringing and setting up a sukkah is work that requires planning. In our modern culture, our idea of travel is in our car, with a suitcase, some small snacks, and credit cards for the restaurants and hotels. For those who are more adventurous, you might bring a self-contained RV, travel trailer, pop-up tent, or a humble cabin tent. You drink bottled water and produce enough litter to fill trash barrels daily. Our idea of "roughing it" is **not** sleeping in our beds at home and having to move a lawn chair away from the smoke of a camp fire because it is in our faces. We do this for a couple of days and call it an "exhausting" vacation.

## HOW MESSIANICS PREPARE FOR THE GREATER EXODUS

Keeping the Feast of Tabernacles forces you to go beyond that. First, you are there for several days and you must develop a daily routine. The days of the week (Monday, Tuesday, etc.) vanish with only Sabbath being the marker for the days. Such will be the case for the *Greater Exodus*. When you are escaping and surviving, minor inconveniences will no longer be important. The Feast of Tabernacles prepares us mentally and practically to quickly adjust to God's plan for our deliverance – the *Greater Exodus*.

If you would like to learn from others what is learned in keeping the Feast of Tabernacles, Lion and Lamb Ministries offers another text entitled The Tribulation Handbook. It is full of lessons learned from keeping the feast. It offers instruction on how to coordinate your camp with others, and it has an extensive appendix listing things to bring when you "plunder Egypt" and actually start the *Greater Exodus*. When Moses concluded his final discourse in the Book of Deuteronomy, he spoke of the Feast of Tabernacles, asking that the Torah be read publicly for all of Israel to hear. He then concluded his discourse by saying,

> *For it* [his last teaching] *is not an idle word for you; indeed it is your life* [your very survival].
> 
> **Deuteronomy 32:47a**

TWELVE

# THE TWO HOUSES OF ISRAEL IN THE GREATER EXODUS

Many of the passages addressing the subject of the *Greater Exodus* also refer to another subject of eschatology called "Restoring the Two Houses of Israel." Bible students are aware of the history of Israel after Kings David and Solomon, when the nation of Israel split into two kingdoms.

The ten northern tribes, under the leadership of Jeroboam, an Ephraimite, led to a separation from the leadership of the House of David. It was your typical tax revolt. After Solomon's death, the northern tribes asked to have their taxes reduced. During his reign, Solomon had levied taxes for the construction of the temple and other major building projects. The new young king of Judah (Rehoboam) counseled with his father's elder counselors first, then with young men with whom he had grown up. The older counselors recommended that the taxes be lowered; the younger said the taxes should be raised. The king chose the counsel of the younger men and the northern tribes rebelled (1 Kings 12:1-20).

A civil war could have developed, but instead, the two kingdoms were simply divided and began to take on their own individual characteristics. The northern kingdom became known as the *House of Israel*, and they proceeded to replicate the temple in

## THE TWO HOUSES OF ISRAEL IN THE GREATER EXODUS

Jerusalem by building imitations in Bethel and Dan. The foundation of one of these temples still stands in the land of Israel at Tel Dan. The Ephraimite king of Israel did not want the people traveling all the way to Jerusalem to worship the Lord, so he built substitute temples. What was worse, he installed Sumerian gods (godlike bulls) in the inner sanctuaries and carried on their own temple worship. Once Israel was taken captive by the Assyrians, the Samaritans dominated the northern lands. The southern kingdom became known as the *House of Judah*, and they became very parochial with the temple in Jerusalem. After the Babylonian exile and return, the Jewish religious leadership in Jerusalem became bigoted and restricted worship in the temple to only Jews and some Israelites.

Various biblical prophets were sent by God to one or both kingdoms. For example, the Prophet Hosea (one of the first) was sent to the House of Israel. Isaiah was a prophet sent to Judah. In fact, to understand the major and minor prophets of the Bible you must understand the two houses of Israel and its resulting history.

The prophets of Israel spoke to their fellow citizens in the midst of division, rebellion, and God's judgments pointing out their disobedience to God and warning of their impending exile to the nations. Hosea spoke to the House of Israel warning them of exile to the Assyrians, while Jeremiah spoke to the House of Judah and their exile to Babylon. Isaiah also warned Judah of worldwide exile. Additionally, these prophets prophesied something else together. They spoke of a future when God would bring all of them back together again from the nations to become the "whole House of Israel." Many times this reunion is called "Restoring the House of Jacob."

We should note a very subtle thing that exists in Scripture when it uses the names "Jacob" and "Israel." This is not an absolute,

## THE TWO HOUSES OF ISRAEL IN THE GREATER EXODUS

but there is a trend in Scripture that when the name "Jacob" is used the remnant of Israel is in the nations; whereas, the name "Israel" is used whenever the remnant is traveling to the promised land or are in the land. The first instance of this is when Jacob wrestled the Angel just before entering the promised land. His name was changed to "Israel" then.

Turning back to the timing of the future reunion of the whole House of Jacob/Israel, it is integrated into the events at the end of the ages, including the great tribulation, the *day of the* LORD, and the start of the Messianic kingdom and age.

You would think that this topic would fall right in line with other eschatology subjects taught by many, taking its rightful place with them, but such is not the case. There is great emotion in talking about this subject. It tends to rub against other theologies, rubbing them raw.

*Replacement theology* dismisses any teaching that would suggest a future for Israel. According to this erroneous theology, all those prophecies are spiritualized into good things for the church. Others with a *dispensational* outlook ignore the implications and the breadth of the subject only to bring back a national Israel, but on dual tracks—Israel and the church. Many pro-Israel groups hold and favor this position. They virtually ignore that there is a House of Israel still to return. Within the modern Messianic movement this is a very "raw" topic.

The modern state of Israel is without question the "House of Judah," but some Messianic Jews associated with the large national organizations believe that the House of Israel was rejoined to Judah in the ancient past and there is no more future prophecy of a restoration, except for Jews. They claim that the prophecies of Ephraim joining Judah were fulfilled when the remnant of Judah returned from Babylonian captivity. All of Israel is called

"Jews" now. They believe there is no future reunion of the House of Israel with the House of Judah.

This is an interesting dilemma for those Messianic Jews. They claim that they are the true witnesses of Yeshua to their fellow Jews, but Judaism does believe there is a future reunion of the Two Houses. Supporting Judaism on this point, the Bible says that Judah will be brought back *first* from worldwide captivity, hence we have the modern nation of Israel, and in the midst of a time period called "Jacob's trouble" the House of Israel will return and join with the House of Judah.

> *"For, behold, days are coming," declares the LORD, "when I will restore the fortunes of My people Israel and Judah." The LORD says, "I will also bring them back to the land that I gave to their forefathers, and they shall possess it." Now these are the words which the LORD spoke concerning Israel and concerning Judah: For thus says the LORD, "I have heard a sound of terror, of dread, and there is no peace. Ask now, and see, if a male can give birth. Why do I see every man with his hands on his loins, as a woman in childbirth? And why have all faces turned pale? Alas! For that day is great, there is none like it; and it is the time of Jacob's distress* [trouble]*, but he will be saved from it."* **Jeremiah 30:3-7**

*Jacob's trouble* (distress) concerns the end times, not the ancient past. It is Ezekiel who best describes the modern state of Israel, born out of the Holocaust, and presents the prophecies of the two houses of Israel.

> *The hand of the LORD was upon me, and He brought me out by the Spirit of the LORD and set me down in the middle of the valley; and it was full of bones. He caused me to pass among them round about, and behold, there were very*

*many on the surface of the valley; and lo, they were very dry. He said to me, "Son of man, can these bones live?" And I answered, "O Lord G*OD*, You know." Again He said to me, "Prophesy over these bones, and say to them, 'O dry bones, hear the word of the L*ORD*.' Thus says the Lord G*OD *to these bones, 'Behold, I will cause breath to enter you that you may come to life. I will put sinews on you, make flesh grow back on you, cover you with skin, and put breath in you that you may come alive; and you will know that I am the L*ORD*.'" So I prophesied as I was commanded; and as I prophesied, there was a noise, and behold, a rattling; and the bones came together, bone to its bone. And I looked, and behold, sinews were on them, and flesh grew, and skin covered them; but there was no breath in them. Then He said to me, "Prophesy to the breath, prophesy, son of man, and say to the breath, 'Thus says the Lord G*OD*, "Come from the four winds, O breath, and breathe on these slain, that they come to life."'" So I prophesied as He commanded me, and the breath came into them, and they came to life, and stood on their feet, an exceedingly great army.* **Ezekiel 37:1-10**

This prophecy has been quoted many times, even by Messianic Jews, to explain how the modern nation of Israel has been born out ashes. Today, modern Israel stands strong surrounded by enemies that suffer greatly if they attempt to harm Israel. It is as Zechariah spoke.

> *"Behold, I am going to make Jerusalem a cup that causes reeling to all the peoples around; and when the siege is against Jerusalem, it will also be against Judah. It will come about in that day that I will make Jerusalem a heavy stone for all the peoples; all who lift it will be severely injured. And all the nations of the earth will be gathered against it. In that day," declares the* L*ORD*, *"I will strike*

*every horse with bewilderment, and his rider with madness. But I will watch over the house of Judah, while I strike every horse of the peoples with blindness. Then the clans of Judah will say in their hearts, 'A strong support for us are the inhabitants of Jerusalem through the* L<small>ORD</small> *of hosts, their God.' In that day I will make the clans of Judah like a firepot among pieces of wood and a flaming torch among sheaves, so they will consume on the right hand and on the left all the surrounding peoples, while the inhabitants of Jerusalem again dwell on their own sites in Jerusalem. The* L<small>ORD</small> *also will save the tents of Judah first so that the glory of the house of David and the glory of the inhabitants of Jerusalem will not be magnified above Judah."* **Zechariah 12:2-7**

Virtually all evangelical Christians and Messianic Jews agree that these words describe our present day. But going back to Ezekiel, the dry bones prophecy was not exclusively for Judah. He further defines how the House of Israel will be part of it also. He even uses the language of the end of the ages, the final redemption, and the resurrection!

*Then He said to me, "Son of man, these bones are the whole house of Israel; behold, they say, 'Our bones are dried up, and our hope has perished. We are completely cut off.' Therefore prophesy, and say to them, 'Thus says the Lord G*<small>OD</small>*, "Behold, I will open your graves and cause you to come up out of your graves, My people; and I will bring you into the land of Israel. Then you will know that I am the* L<small>ORD</small>*, when I have opened your graves and caused you to come up out of your graves, My people. I will put My Spirit within you, and you will come to life, and I will place you on your own land. Then you will know that I, the* L<small>ORD</small>*, have spoken and done it," declares the* L<small>ORD</small>*.'"*
**Ezekiel 37:11-14**

# THE TWO HOUSES OF ISRAEL IN THE GREATER EXODUS

This is God's end-time goal, gathering the tribes of Israel from the nations back to the promised land. He will also raise all of His saints from the dead to live with Him for eternity. Ezekiel begins to explain how the House of Israel joins the House of Judah. Those who oppose the two-house teaching undercut key prophecies about the restoration and how the two houses are joined at the *Greater Exodus*.

> *The word of the* L*ord* *came again to me saying, "And you, son of man, take for yourself one stick and write on it, 'For Judah and for the sons of Israel, his companions'; then take another stick and write on it, 'For Joseph, the stick of Ephraim and all the house of Israel, his companions.' Then join them for yourself one to another into one stick, that they may become one in your hand. When the sons of your people speak to you saying, 'Will you not declare to us what you mean by these?' say to them, 'Thus says the Lord* G*od*, *"Behold, I will take the stick of Joseph, which is in the hand of Ephraim, and the tribes of Israel, his companions; and I will put them with it, with the stick of Judah, and make them one stick, and they will be one in My hand."' The sticks on which you write will be in your hand before their eyes. Say to them, 'Thus says the Lord* G*od*, *"Behold, I will take the sons of Israel from among the nations where they have gone, and I will gather them from every side and bring them into their own land; and I will make them one nation in the land, on the mountains of Israel; and one king will be king for all of them; and they will no longer be two nations and no longer be divided into two kingdoms."'* **Ezekiel 37:15-22**

The prophecy states that Ephraim (Israel) would be joined with Judah. Therefore, Judah must be in the land first before Ephraim can join them. Furthermore, Judah already follows the teachings of Moses. Ephraim joining Judah includes a return to Mosaic teaching.

Ezekiel was a prophet in Babylon during the captivity of Judah to Babylon. However, Judaism does not teach that this prophecy was fulfilled when the remnant of Judah returned from Babylon. To this day it is regarded as a future prophecy. It may be that, in this modern Messianic movement, many of the persons of "non-Jewish" descent are in fact the House of Israel joining the House of Judah. We don't know that with any certainty, but we do know that these "non Jews" are turning back to the Torah and remembering Moses. This is just as Ezekiel said.

*They* [those joining] *will no longer defile themselves with their idols, or with their detestable things, or with any of their transgressions; but I will deliver them from all their dwelling places in which they have sinned, and will cleanse them. And they will be My people, and I will be their God.*
**Ezekiel 37:23**

This three-part repentance of turning away from idols, not eating the detestable, and not transgressing the commandments is virtually identical to the "letter to the Gentiles" cited in Acts 15:22-29. This was the counsel given expressly for believing Gentiles who were coming to the New Covenant faith in the Messiah. Ezekiel does not leave out the believing Gentiles in the two houses coming together either.

Both Judah and Ephraim are described as having companions. These companions are "believing Gentiles" from the various nations that the *Greater Exodus* collects as well. This is just like the Egyptian exodus. Those who left Egypt were a mixed multitude. Both native and alien (other slaves from other peoples) were mixed and they were numbered in the tribes of Israel. They were not segregated. Therefore, we can conclude that when God restores the two houses of Israel, others (believing Gentiles) will join with them in this fulfillment. They are to follow the same Torah commandments given to the native born. This is just as

Moses taught in the mixed multitude of the children of Israel concerning the aliens and sojourners.

> *"As for the assembly, there shall be one statute for you and for the alien who sojourns with you, a perpetual statute throughout your generations; as you are, so shall the alien be before the Lord. There is to be one law and one ordinance for you and for the alien who sojourns with you."*
> **Numbers 15:15-16**

The same Messianic Jews who dispute the two houses also dispute that the Torah should be taught to non-Jews. They are going to be shocked when the *Greater Exodus* occurs. Hosea is one of the first prophets who wrote of the unique way that the House of Israel would come back from worldwide captivity. I say *unique* because the worldwide exile of Israel was much different from that of Judah. Let me explain. Hosea had three children and the names given to them laid out God's judgment for the House of Israel.

Hosea's children were named Jezreel, Lo-ruhamah, and Lo-ammi. Jezreel means "scattered." The large valley in Northern Israel is called the "Jezreel Valley" where seed is scattered and where much of the grain of Israel is grown. Hosea prophesied that the House of Israel would be "scattered" throughout the nations.

Next, Lo-ruhamah means "no compassion." Hosea said that the House of Israel would not receive any compassion from the Lord while they were scattered. He would turn His face away and not give attention to their cries for help.

Finally, Lo-ammi means "not my people." Hosea said that the House of Israel would lose their identity with the land of Israel and as individual tribes (Israelites). This has truly happened to the northern tribes, sometimes referred to as the "lost tribes" (see

Luke 19:10, Matthew 15:24, and Matthew 10:6). They have lost their ancestral identification and are somewhat surprised to think they might even belong to Israel or be any part of the LORD's covenant with native Israel. Still further, the idea of returning to Judah is not that appealing to them.

When the prophecy speaks of the reunion of the two houses, it is not talking about everyone becoming Jewish. Both houses are joined together because they both seek the same God of Israel, not Israel to become Jewish, yet many Jews think that. So what does joining Judah really mean?

Answer: It has to do with the teaching of the Torah and the promise of the land. This is how Hosea, described joining with Judah.

> *Yet the number of the sons of Israel will be like the sand of the sea, which cannot be measured or numbered; and in the place where it is said to them, "You are not My people," it will be said to them, "You are the sons of the living God." And the sons of Judah and the sons of Israel will be gathered together, and they will appoint for themselves one leader, and they will go up from the land, for great will be the day of Jezreel.* **Hosea 1:10-11**

The phrase the *sons of the living God* is a very New Covenant expression tied to Peter's confession of faith in Yeshua when he said, "*You are the Son of the Living God.*" (Matthew 16:16) Christians today refer to themselves as "sons of the Living God." Hosea uses this expression to describe how the House of Israel would return in faith at the end of days. The appointment of a single leader (the Messiah) is further evidence of belief in Messiah Yeshua. The final reference to the *day of Jezreel* is another expression of the *day of the LORD*. The valley of Jezreel is bordered on the southern edge by a mountain, called "Har Meggido." You may be more familiar with the name "Armageddon." The battle of Armageddon is the final element in the great tribulation and the *day of the* LORD.

At this present time, the Israeli *Law of Return* only allows "Jews" to enter the land as citizens. Non-Jews (candidates for the House of Israel) are not recognized as a cohesive element of Israel as they defer to being a physical descendant from a Jewish mother. But within Israel there is a sense of anticipation concerning non-Jews wanting to emigrate, and they are referred to as "B'nai Ephraim" (the sons of Ephraim). What will bring about their return from exile and begin the process of joining with Judah? When will the Law of Return welcome Ephraim? The answer to that is still in the future, but the prophet Ezekiel offers some evidence toward this answer when he addresses the *Greater Exodus*. It comes about at the end of a regional war with modern Israel. The nations to the north of Israel are to attack and invade the mountains of Israel. It will result in a stunning victory for Israel. The battle is described in Ezekiel 38 and 39 concluding with these words.

> *And I will set My glory among the nations; and all the nations will see My judgment which I have executed, and My hand which I have laid on them. And the house of Israel will know that I am the* LORD *their God from that day onward.* **Ezekiel 39:21-22**

This particular battle will be the stage set for God to step into the modern world in a very dramatic way. He will use this victory to command the attention of the world and show Himself strong on behalf of Israel, just as He did with Pharaoh and Egypt. The lesson of the *Greater Exodus* is all about "knowing the LORD," just as it was in the Egyptian exodus.

> *"The nations will know that the house of Israel went into exile for their iniquity because they acted treacherously*

> *against Me, and I hid My face from them; so I gave them into the hand of their adversaries, and all of them fell by the sword. According to their uncleanness and according to their transgressions I dealt with them, and I hid My face from them." Therefore thus says the Lord G*OD*, "Now I will restore the fortunes of Jacob, and have mercy on the whole house of Israel; and I will be jealous for My holy name. They will forget their disgrace and all their treachery which they perpetrated against Me, when they live securely on their own land with no one to make them afraid. When I bring them back from the peoples and gather them from the lands of their enemies, then I shall be sanctified through them in the sight of the many nations. Then they will know that I am the L*ORD *their God because I made them go into exile among the nations, and then gathered them again to their own land; and I will leave none of them there any longer. I will not hide My face from them any longer, for I will have poured out My Spirit on the house of Israel," declares the Lord G*OD*.* **Ezekiel 39:23-29**

Just as Moses and Ezekiel said earlier, Israel would be returning after a national repentance, then the House of Israel is to realize who they are and why they were cast into the nations. Hosea's prophecy of judgment will also be reversed. Instead of "scattered," they will be brought back. Instead of "no compassion," God will turn His face toward them. Instead of "not My people," God will pour out His Spirit upon them. With the Spirit, both Houses will suddenly have eyes that see and ears that hear. These things will happen after God is shown strong on Israel's behalf against their enemies. The drama will be palpable.

One of the best known parables of Yeshua is the return of the Prodigal Son. It mimics the prophecy of the House of Israel joining Judah at the end of the ages. The parable describes a disobedient son (the House of Israel) who departs from his father and older brother. But then the son suffers great loss away from home among the Gentiles. He humbly returns to his father's house where his older brother still lives; whereupon, the father receives him with joy and holds a feast, serving a fatted calf. The older son is resentful, complaining that he has remained faithful to his father and his household but has not been given so much as a goat for a feast.

The sacrifices for the feasts are directly connected to the house of Israel and the house of Judah with the return of Ephraim, the Prodigal Son. The symbol for the tribe of Ephraim is a "bull calf." The common sacrifice of the Jews in the House of the LORD was a "goat." The story is not just about a sinful young man returning from his worldly ways. It is also about resolving the conflict between two brothers in that house. The House of Israel (Ephraim) rejected the other house. The House of Judah wants to put Ephraim under subjection when they return. Resolving these issues are necessary for the two houses to be united, just as Isaiah says.

> *Then the jealousy of Ephraim will depart, and those who harass Judah will be cut off; Ephraim will not be jealous of Judah, and Judah will not harass Ephraim.* **Isaiah 11:13**

The schism between the Messianic Jews and those who call themselves "Ephraimites" will also be resolved. I know it should not be, but today in the modern Messianic movement, envy and strife exists on this very matter. One national Messianic Jewish organization published a white paper entitled the "Ephraimite Error" in an effort to suppress Messianic "non-Jews" from asserting their possible Israelite heritage. It is nothing less than racial bigotry and ignores the prophetic restoration of the whole House of Jacob. However, I believe this schism will be healed when God pours out His Spirit on all of us and assembles the camp of the righteous at the *Greater Exodus*. This ancient family split must be healed in the wilderness before we can be gathered together to enter the kingdom.

Those who resist the restoration of the two houses of Israel are blind to the prophecies and will most likely not be those who escape, survive, and endure to the end. It is not wise to be ignorant of God's great plan for the remnant in our days. Remember the lesson from the past. Not everyone who left Egypt, even with the blood of the Lamb on their doorposts, made it into the promised land. Those who were at odds with God died along the way. In the same way, despite our present testimony of the Messiah, if we are at odds with God's plan for the *Greater Exodus*, don't expect to escape, survive, and endure to walk into the kingdom.

THIRTEEN

# TRANSITIONING TO TRIBES IN THE CAMP

When the children of Israel fled Egypt, it was a traumatic event for them. Despite seeing the judgments fall upon the Egyptians and not them, with the assurances of Moses and Aaron, and with the promises of God given to Abraham, the children of Israel endured upheaval. After multiple generations, the children of Israel were slaves and did not know how to be free men. As slaves, one of their greatest fears was how Pharaoh might react. While in Egypt, Moses announced that God would soon take them to the promised land. However, the people were despondent. In retaliation to Moses, Pharaoh made them make bricks without straw. At the Red Sea, the children of Israel found themselves blocked by the sea and the mountains with the chariots of Pharaoh bearing down on them. With the exception of Moses, there was no leadership per se in the camp and panic set in. They feared the wrath of Pharaoh. They responded immediately by blaming Moses for having brought them out of Egypt.

> *Then they said to Moses, "Is it because there were no graves in Egypt that you have taken us away to die in the wilderness? Why have you dealt with us in this way, bringing us out of Egypt? Is this not the word that we spoke to you in Egypt, saying, 'Leave us alone that we may serve the Egyptians'? For it would have been better for us to serve the Egyptians than to die in the wilderness."* ***Exodus 14:11-12***

## TRANSITIONING TO TRIBES IN THE CAMP

Let's step into the sandals of the Israelites for a moment. Their situation was virtually impossible. From a tactical standpoint, they had no escape route. People were in a state of panic and on the brink of harming one another before Pharaoh could reach them. Pharaoh had sent his elite military force – his chariots.

Pharaoh's chariots were a well known military weapons system and were considered to be the leading edge of military science in that day. Lightweight, carrying two men, and pulled by two horses, these chariots could run down and out-maneuver any combat force. They were also armed with Egyptian composite bows (a powerful bow used to this day) and supplied with several quivers of arrows. If they wanted to engage a force at long-range, they would stop the chariot and fire arrows up to 250 yards away. Or, if they wanted to carry out a "lightning attack," one would drive the chariot while the other fired from it. This was a very successful "hit and run" that proved devastating in battle. Once they ran out of arrows or had overwhelmed the opposition, they could dismount the chariots and fight with swords hand to hand. The men who manned these chariots were the most skilled of Pharaoh's soldiers on the level of our modern day Marines and special forces. Had Pharaoh's chariots launched an attack, they would have slaughtered the Israelites while suffering very few, if any, casualties.

At the height of the concern, Moses responded with this:

> *But Moses said to the people, "Do not fear! Stand by and see the salvation of the LORD which He will accomplish for you today; for the Egyptians whom you have seen today, you will never see them again forever. The LORD will fight for you while you keep silent."* **Exodus 14:13-14**

Torah teachers use Moses' statement to interpret what was the nature and diversity of the panic. For example, they teach that four diverse responses were in the camp. The first was suicidal. They believed that many of the people were willing to throw themselves into the sea and drown, instead of being struck by spears, arrows, or swords. The second response was surrender. They believed that many of the people were willing to immediately prostrate themselves before Pharaoh and return as slaves forever. The third response is almost bizarre. They believed that many of the people were nonreactive, ignoring the problem all together, like nothing was happening and believed their inaction would result in them being ignored by Pharaoh. The final response was fighting in self-defense! They believed that many were ready to take up whatever arms they had and fight it out.

Moses' statement seems to answer these four responses of the people.
**Suicidal:** *Do not fear!*
**Surrender:** *Stand by and see the salvation of the LORD which He will accomplish for you today*
**Nonreactive:** *you will never see them again forever*
**Fighting:** *The LORD will fight for you while you keep silent.*

The LORD delayed Pharaoh's chariots with the pillar of fire, opened the Red Sea, and Israel escaped in the night, walking on dry land through the midst of the sea. Once they were on the other side (it took them all night), then Pharaoh rushed in, only to have the LORD close the path through the sea. Israel was saved and Pharaoh's chariots were sunk and his horses and their riders were drowned. The most elite soldiers of the world's foremost military force were wiped out in a matter of minutes while the Israelites looked on.

> *Thus the LORD saved Israel that day from the hand of the Egyptians, and Israel saw the Egyptians dead on the seashore.* **Exodus 14:30**

## TRANSITIONING TO TRIBES IN THE CAMP

Consider what the *Greater Exodus* may include. Before the great tribulation and the start of the *Greater Exodus*, we may find ourselves "making bricks without straw" as the governments of the nations we live in become oppressive toward us and our faith. Many western nations have already started moving in that direction. And, if suddenly, we leave the cities en masse contrary to their desires, they could try to bring us back. It is a fact that the U.S. government wants all lawful citizens to be in relocation and "re-educational" centers in case of any perceived emergency. According to Homeland Security documentation, relocation centers will be used to bring in all citizens to the large cities to facilitate the logistics of the emergency plan. They have also done "threat assessments" and believe that many citizens will not cooperate with emergency plans and procedures. Soldiers and Homeland Security personnel have been trained to accomplish their task and have been told that persons refusing to follow these emergency orders should be considered as hostile and dangerous. Conservative citizens and "Doomsday Preppers" are at the top of this list. I am sure that many of the brethren in the camps will be fearful and concerned about leaving their homes and what may result. It is more than possible that many believers will experience the same four reactions like at the Red Sea when the time for the *Greater Exodus* begins.

Once Pharaoh's chariots were soundly defeated, the children of Israel were faced with a shortage of food. They quickly compared what they formerly had in Egypt (*"...we ate bread to the full"* Exodus 16:3) to what they had now (essentially nothing) in the wilderness. God then gave them manna (*"It is the bread which the* LORD *has given you to eat."* Exodus 16:15) and instructed them to keep the Sabbath (*"See, the* LORD *has given you the Sabbath;..."* Exodus 16:29). From there, the people traveled and ran out of water. So, their complaints turned into quarreling with Moses. With direction from the LORD, Moses took his staff and struck the Rock, providing water for the people

## TRANSITIONING TO TRIBES IN THE CAMP

and their animals. The people's quarrel resulted in a clear test of the LORD—(*"Is the LORD among us, or not?"* Exodus 17:7). Then Amalek, a nation of raiders and bandits in the wilderness, came and attacked the stragglers and those along the edges of the camp. The children of Israel were forced to choose men, and Joshua led this force against Amalek. Once that battle was fought, the children of Israel traveled near to the mountain of the burning bush. It was then that the leadership structure of the camp came into question. Quite simply, Moses was making all of the decisions and there was a bottleneck. Upon Yithro's (Moses' father-in-law) counsel, Moses began to delegate his authority and the leadership of the camp.

> *Furthermore, you shall select out of all the people able men who fear God, men of truth, those who hate dishonest gain; and you shall place these over them, as leaders of thousands, of hundreds, of fifties and of tens.* **Exodus 18:21**

> *And Moses chose able men out of all Israel, and made them heads over the people, leaders of thousands, of hundreds, of fifties and of tens.* **Exodus 18:25**

From there the leadership of each of the tribes began to take shape.

> *With you, moreover, there shall be a man of each tribe, each one head of his father's household. These then are the names of the men who shall stand with you: of Reuben, Elizur the son of Shedeur; of Simeon, Shelumiel the son of Zurishaddai; of Judah, Nahshon the son of Amminadab; of Issachar, Nethanel the son of Zuar; of Zebulun, Eliab the son of Helon; of the sons of Joseph: of Ephraim, Elishama the son of Ammihud; of Manasseh, Gamaliel the son of Pedahzur; of Benjamin, Abidan the son of Gideoni; of Dan, Ahiezer the son of Ammishaddai; of Asher, Pagiel the son of Ochran; of Gad, Eliasaph the son of Deuel; of*

## TRANSITIONING TO TRIBES IN THE CAMP

*Naphtali, Ahira the son of Enan. These are they who were called of the congregation, the leaders of their fathers' tribes; they were the heads of divisions of Israel.*
***Numbers 1:4-16***

Now let us step back and see the pattern that occurred in the early days and months of the exodus. First, the people were afraid of everything. This produced panic and set the camp on the edge of self-destruction. Second, the lack of basics for life, such as food and water, caused the people to be openly contentious with Moses and God. Finally, the need for organization, the delegation of authority, and sharing the burden of leadership became obvious. The calamity seemed to end when the leadership in the camp was established. Real complaints could be serviced. The lines of communication in the camp were clear. You didn't need to out-shout someone to be heard. The leadership in the camp was at the tribal level. Moses was no longer the single leader of the camp. Instead, he shared the direction from the LORD with the tribal leaders, then the tribal leaders instructed the subordinate leaders, who then carryied out the instruction. Communication was actually enhanced and accelerated. Feedback from the people made it to the leaders and decision makers faster. Among the tribes, there were specific assignments as to where the tribes camped, which tribes were stationed as the vanguard element, which tribes guarded the flanks, and which tribes had the rear guard. The Scriptures say that the tribes traveled in "martial array" (Exodus 13:18). *Martial array* is a militaristic term denoting great organization and capability. Tribal government enhanced their ability to defend themselves and protect their wives and children in the camp.

Let us fast-forward now into the future. Assume for the moment that the exile of the nations has been concluded by God and He has poured out His Spirit upon the whole House of Israel worldwide. God has now taken steps to restore the House of Jacob and

## TRANSITIONING TO TRIBES IN THE CAMP

bring the two houses of Israel together. At the same time, it is the season of winter and the events of the great tribulation unfold with the Abomination of Desolation happening. Then those in Judea flee to the wilderness and those who are going to escape in the nations (the Remnant) sit down to the final Passover seder in their homes. Elijah (or "one in the spirit of Elijah") has begun to testify at the cold altar, and those observing know this is the Passover seder that starts the *Greater Exodus*. Then upon completion of the Passover, they gather their families and their sukkah and head for the *wilderness of the peoples* to join the camp of their like-minded brethren during the days of the Feast of Unleavened Bread. For seven days, while eating the "bread of haste" (matzot) they assemble with many others where they have previously practiced the Feast of Tabernacles. What can they expect in that first camp called Sukkot?

They can expect a mixture of joy and excitement, fear and trepidation. The joy and excitement will be the reality of finally coming to the final days of this age and living at the edge of immortality and the Messianic Age. The fear and trepidation will be the issues that the ancients experienced. It won't be long before adequate provisions and security of the camp comes to the forefront for everyone. If these concerns are not addressed quickly and correctly, the camp will become an uncivilized disaster. The very first lessons of the wilderness will make or break the camps early on.

The God of Israel knows this and has a plan for us in the *Greater Exodus*. He is going to re-establish the tribes of Israel with specific leaders by name for each camp. It will begin with the sealing of the 144,000. The sealing must take place prior to any of God's judgments upon the physical elements of the earth (Revelation 7:1-3). It will most likely happen quickly after the camp is filled with brethren. The actual individual sealings will be done by an angel and is described by the prophet Ezekiel.

## TRANSITIONING TO TRIBES IN THE CAMP

*Behold, six men came from the direction of the upper gate which faces north, each with his shattering weapon in his hand; and among them was a certain man clothed in linen with a writing case at his loins. And they went in and stood beside the bronze altar. Then the glory of the God of Israel went up from the cherub on which it had been, to the threshold of the temple. And He called to the man clothed in linen at whose loins was the writing case. The LORD said to him, "Go through the midst of the city, even through the midst of Jerusalem, and put a mark on the foreheads of the men who sigh and groan over all the abominations which are being committed in its midst." ...Then behold, the man clothed in linen at whose loins was the writing case reported, saying, "I have done just as You hast commanded me."*
**Ezekiel 9:2-4, 11**

Apparently, the seal in the forehead of the 144,000 is a visible sign (Revelation 7:3-4). It is believed that God's name (YHVH) will be written in some manner on their foreheads. The 144,000 are divided by tribe with 12,000 from each. It appears that everyone in the same tribe is sealed on the same day, regardless of where they are in the world. The sealing appears to be a 12 day process. Additionally, those sealed are very concerned about the events happening throughout the world and understand that the great tribulation is presently underway. The Scriptures say that they sigh and groan at the abominations. This is from the testimony of Ezekiel who described the sealing process of the 144,000 (Ezekiel 9). Consider this possibility; once the sealing is completed, there may be a representative of each tribe present in every camp, causing at least 12 of the 144,000 to be present in every camp. If that plan is correct, there could be as many as 12,000 camps worldwide. Regardless of how they are dispersed, I believe each tribe will be sealed on one particular day in the sequence given in Revelation 7:5-8 (12,000 from Judah on the first day, on the second day 12,000 from Reuben, 12,000 from Gad

## TRANSITIONING TO TRIBES IN THE CAMP

on the third day, 12,000 from Asher on the fourth day, 12,000 from Naphtali on the fifth day, 12,000 from Manasseh on the sixth day, 12,000 from Simeon on the seventh day, 12,000 from Levi on the eighth day, 12,000 from Issachar on the ninth day, 12,000 from Zebulun on the tenth day, 12,000 from Joseph on the eleventh day, and 12,000 from the tribe of Benjamin on the 12th day). This plan of sealing (one tribe each day) is consistent with something else that happened in the ancient exodus.

When the ancients set up the tabernacle, they dedicated and sealed the altar with one tribe coming each day to offer gifts of dedication. It was a 12 day process. The pattern of the sealing and dedication of the altar in the wilderness is the same pattern of sealing and dedicating the 144,000 in the *Greater Exodus*. The process and the gifts are described in the Book of Numbers.

> *Then the* LORD *said to Moses, "Let them present their offering, one leader each day, for the dedication of the altar." Now the one who presented his offering on the first day was Nahshon the son of Amminadab, of the tribe of Judah;...* **Numbers 7:11-12**

In the *Greater Exodus*, the altar has been shut down in Jerusalem. The altar is not sealed and dedicated. This time, God seals and dedicates the tribes (12,000 each) wherever they are scattered in the earth. Still further, there is an exciting promise given by the Messiah concerning the matter of re-establishing the tribes and tribal government.

In Revelation chapters two and three, seven "churches" (defined as called out assemblies) are offered correction and promises from the Messiah. These messages are given to make final preparation before the great tribulation and *Greater Exodus* occur. In particular, the church of Pergamum is given a promise as follows:

## TRANSITIONING TO TRIBES IN THE CAMP

*He who has an ear, let him hear what the Spirit says to the churches. To him who overcomes, to him I will give some of the hidden manna, and I will give him a white stone, and a new name written on the stone which no one knows but he who receives it.* **Revelation 2:17**

The *white stone* in this verse could be better translated the *brightly illuminated stone*. The stone in question is referring to the Urim and Thummim that was in the High Priest's ephod (breastplate). We are not certain how they worked, but ancient Jewish sources say the High Priest could pose a question before God and He would answer through these stones. One stone would become brightly illuminated. Urim means "lights." The stone would signal that God was answering while the other stone(s) (Thummim) would give an affirmative or negative response. David consulted these when pursuing the Philistines in a battle and was given the "go ahead." But even more significant is the use of the Urim and Thummim to affirm ancestral heritage. When the remnant of Judah returned from Babylon, there was serious question as to who was a priest and who was of the other tribes. The Urim and Thummim were used to determine ancestral backgrounds. The *white stone* promised to the overcomers by Yeshua could well be used to establish tribal heritages. This determination would be profoundly important in restoring the house of Jacob as He has promised.

In addition, there will also be elders and other overseers in the camp. The ancient camp had distributed leadership (captains of 10's, 100's and 1,000's). This will be necessary for successful tribal authority and government. With this structure in place, the sealed members of the 144,000 would most likely serve as tribal leaders in the camps. Until we are in the camps, we don't know exactly how the leadership will be established, yet one thing is for sure, there will be a need for leadership to manage the burdens of the camp.

## TRANSITIONING TO TRIBES IN THE CAMP

So what will "tribal leadership" mean to the average believer in the camp? Technically, this form of government is a *theocracy*, the government of God, not a democracy. This is the form of government Israel had when they first entered the land. Key decisions were made by "judges." The leadership structure makes key "judgments" with each higher level having authority over the lower level. For example, a leader who is a "captain of tens" could be overruled by a leader who is "captain of hundreds," all the way up to the tribal leaders. Who makes the ultimate decision for the entire camp? Answer: the Lord.

When Korah rose up against Moses' authority over the camp, he complained that Moses was doing "too much" meaning that Moses was "lording it over them." He had a core group of 250 princes agreeing with him, and he was appealing to the camp at large. He wanted the camp to democratically choose him. It led to a great rebellion, and Korah lost his life in the process (Numbers 16:1-35). In a theocracy, the Lord is Lord of the camp and His anointed ones carry out His direction. It is not a democracy with everyone having a vote. There is only one vote – the Lord's. Rebellion in the camp of the Lord will lead to the same result. These are very powerful lessons from the exodus for those in the *Greater Exodus*.

Once the camp is functional and completes its first relocation, the brethren will discover that tribal leadership will actually work for them and be the best form of government in the camp. The work and organization of the camp will not be a miracle in itself; it will be as a result of common sense and good decisions. Justice, the kind defined by the Torah, will keep the camp peaceful and healthy. Democratic principles or mob rule will not be used; therefore, a majority of the camp will be insufficient reason for the camp to judge any matter. Leaders will be concerned about how the majority of the camp feels, but that will only be a component in the righteous decision they make.

## TRANSITIONING TO TRIBES IN THE CAMP

Tribal government, as established by Moses and the ancients, is the government of the future kingdom. Practicing this form of government in the camps will be the final training lesson to live in the Messianic Kingdom.

FOURTEEN

# THE CLOUD BY DAY, THE FIRE BY NIGHT

While this topic has been mentioned earlier as part of the *Greater Exodus*, additional explanation is warranted. Of all the things the children of Israel did in the exodus, there is one thing they did very well. They followed the cloud wherever it led them. God provided this visible sign to lead them on their journeys from Egypt through the wilderness until they reached the land He promised to them. We need to understand this phenomenon better, as part of the *Greater Exodus*. It gives insight as to how the LORD will lead the camps. For some, this concept may seem too fantastic and beyond the reach of reason. But, I would remind you that failing to believe what God had already done in the path is the most worn path of unbelief. God did those fantastic things in the past so that we would believe Him in the day of our trouble.

The cloud is called a *pillar* throughout Scripture, but it could have been a *weather plume* because of its vertical shape. As a purely natural weather phenomenon though, it does not explain how the pillar became fire at night. The *pillar* was able to position itself over the tent of meeting, between the children of Israel and Pharaoh's chariots at the Red sea, and lead the people throughout the wilderness showing them where to camp. The first reference to the pillar is at the first camp site of their forty-year journey.

## THE CLOUD BY DAY, THE FIRE BY NIGHT

*Then they set out from Succoth and camped in Etham on the edge of the wilderness. The* LORD *was going before them in a pillar of cloud by day to lead them on the way, and in a pillar of fire by night to give them light, that they might travel by day and by night. He did not take away the pillar of cloud by day, nor the pillar of fire by night, from before the people.* **Exodus 13:20-22**

Sukkot was the first camping place of the children of Israel when they left Egypt. Apparently, the cloud first appeared during the night and began leading them the next day to the camp called Etham.

It must have been a marvel for this pillar of cloud to appear at the front of the camp. Clouds are normal occurrences, but a cloud that is vertical in shape and moves in front of you and transforms into a fiery light at night would have been very unusual, even supernatural. The cloud was large enough that everyone traveling could see the direction to go. At night, the fire was bright enough to enable the travelers to continue traveling even after the sun had set. It had to have been brighter than full moonlight. Remember, the children of Israel left in the middle of the lunar month (15 Nisan/Aviv), so the moon would have been full and just beginning to wane. God wanted them to have additional light at night.

This pillar of cloud led the Children of Israel toward the Red Sea in the first week when they were eating "unleavened bread." And, as we know, Pharaoh had a change of heart about letting Israel leave and dispatched his chariots to bring them back, catching up to them at the Red Sea. The pillar then did something truly unexpected. Instead of just leading at the front of the camp, the pillar suddenly defended them, positioning itself between the Egyptians and Israel. See how Moses describes this event.

# THE CLOUD BY DAY, THE FIRE BY NIGHT

> *The angel of God, who had been going before the camp of Israel, moved and went behind them; and the pillar of cloud moved from before them and stood behind them. So it came between the camp of Egypt and the camp of Israel; and there was the cloud along with the darkness, yet it gave light at night. Thus the one did not come near the other all night.* **Exodus 14:19-20**

Without a lot of explanation, the pillar of cloud is now understood to be the *Angel of God*. The Angel of God immediately causes one to think of God's power and force to stand against enemies. Cecil B. DeMille, in his movie *The Ten Commandments*, depicted this event with the cloud becoming a barrier of fire throughout the night, allowing Israel to cross the Red Sea. That seems to be the consensus of most Bible teachers, the fire by night not only illuminated the way for Israel to cross, but it blocked Pharaoh's chariots. Then the fire changed back into a pillar of cloud in the morning.

> *At the morning watch, the LORD looked down on the army of the Egyptians through the pillar of fire and cloud and brought the army of the Egyptians into confusion.*
> **Exodus 14:24**

The confusion Moses refers to was caused by God pulling off chariot wheels, causing the Egyptians to drive their chariots with difficulty (verse 25). The Egyptians' advance against Israel became fragmented and highly disorganized. It must have been like a multi-car accident on the freeway with chariots careening in every direction because of the lost wheels. In any case, Pharaoh's chariots found themselves stalled in the crossing path of the Red Sea and the waters' sudden return brought about their demise.

There is another simple but profound spiritual lesson about the pillar of fire in the nighttime that ties back to the Angel of the

LORD. Darkness cannot exist in the presence of light. Darkness flees when light appears. The same is true of God's presence, since He is the Light. God's enemies cannot stand in God's presence either. Therefore, the presence of the Angel of the LORD (in the cloud) prohibited the enemies of God (Pharaoh's chariots) from advancing.

The term "Angel of the LORD" is not truly a singular expression about God. It represents the entire Godhead of the LORD. Throughout Scripture we learn that God definitely has parts and manifests Himself in a plural form. The Father seems to be the Judge, the Son seems to be the Word, and the Holy Spirit seems to teach us and comfort us. The pillar did these same functions at various times, testifying to God's full presence and personality.

Judaism struggles with these different manifestations and the plurality of God. References to angels (divine messengers) and God taking on a man-like form in shape or personality is a struggle to comprehend. This struggle is not made easier by Moses. In the resulting journey to Mount Sinai, God specifically appears and talks to Moses from the cloud.

The children of Israel began to mumble and grumble for the lack of food to eat. In response to this need, the LORD brought quail and manna to the camp, but the LORD's presence was made known at this event by the glory of God appearing in the cloud.

> *It came about as Aaron spoke to the whole congregation of the sons of Israel, that they looked toward the wilderness, and behold, the glory of the LORD appeared in the cloud. And the LORD spoke to Moses, saying, "I have heard the grumblings of the sons of Israel; speak to them, saying, 'At twilight you shall eat meat, and in the morning you shall*

> be filled with bread; and you shall know that I am the LORD your God.'" So it came about at evening that the quails came up and covered the camp, and in the morning there was a layer of dew around the camp. When the layer of dew evaporated, behold, on the surface of the wilderness there was a fine flake-like thing, fine as the frost on the ground. When the sons of Israel saw it, they said to one another, "What is it?" For they did not know what it was. And Moses said to them, "It is the bread which the LORD has given you to eat." **Exodus 16:10-15**

I do not know what was different about the appearance of the cloud that indicated the glory of God. I could speculate and say that the cloud may have become very bright, but it is clear that the LORD wanted Israel to know that the quail and manna were from Him and not just happenstance. So, the Angel of the LORD in the cloud manifested Himself to convince the people of His provision and protection. This cloud is more than a novel way to lead Israel in the wilderness; the presence of God was in the cloud leading them. This is the basis for our expectation of a cloud leading the camps in the *Greater Exodus*.

Israel spent almost a year at the base of Mount Sinai. There is not a lot of explanation about the cloud itself during that time. Instead, the Scriptures speak of the LORD coming down onto Mount Sinai in a large cloud and fire on the mountain. However, that cloud was very dark and ominous looking. It served more as a warning to not go up the mountain and it shielded the people from God's power. What is clear though, is God's use of a cloud for His presence.

> The LORD said to Moses, "Behold, I will come to you in a thick cloud, so that the people may hear when I speak with you and may also believe in you forever." Then Moses told the words of the people to the LORD. **Exodus 19:9**

## THE CLOUD BY DAY, THE FIRE BY NIGHT

The LORD God Almighty spoke from the mountain followed by Moses going up the mountain to receive the two tablets of God's commandments. Here we could ask, did the cloud that led Israel to Mount Sinai join with the cloud on the mountain or did it just stand by waiting for events on the mountain? We really don't know, but I would speculate that the cloud and the fire on the mountain was a very specific thing warranting awe, while the pillar by day and fire by night may have remained in place (meaning: stay camped here) and still served as the light by night for the camp.

Between the LORD giving the Torah at Mount Sinai and the erection of the tabernacle, there was a significant negative event that we should consider. While Moses was on the mountain, a group of Israelites rose up against the LORD and made the golden calf as a replacement god. Moses later returned with the tablets of God's law, threw them down in anger upon witnessing the idolatry, and those who worshipped the calf were slaughtered (about 3,000 of them).

There is a lot of commentary on how this tragedy occurred. How could they have done this, having just left Egypt with all of its judgments, crossing the Red Sea, and witnessing God speak to them from atop the mountain giving the Ten Commandments?

How could they make the golden calf with the cloud still present with them every day and the light at night was still there? We can extend that question to other mistakes that took place in the wilderness. The cloud was present every day, yet it did not seem to deter their negative behavior against Moses or the LORD.

It seems that the presence of the cloud became commonplace in the minds of the Israelites and did not seem to register as significant to them as time went on. I find this disturbing because many of us today regard the Holy Spirit (God's presence to lead us) in the same manner as Israel did the cloud. When the pillar of cloud leads the *Greater Exodus*, will the tribulation saints make the same mistake?

There was a daily routine in the presence of the cloud for forty years, and Israel just learned to check the condition of the cloud and go on with their daily activities.

> *Throughout all their journeys whenever the cloud was taken up from over the tabernacle, the sons of Israel would set out; but if the cloud was not taken up, then they did not set out until the day when it was taken up. For throughout all their journeys, the cloud of the* Lord *was on the tabernacle by day, and there was fire in it by night, in the sight of all the house of Israel.* **Exodus 40:36-38**

Hopefully, the tribulation saints will not make the same mistakes as the ancients did. Consider the difference this time. The tribulation saints have the history of the exodus, the rebels will be weeded out of the camp by the Lord directly, and members of the 144,000 will be in the camps. Israel's exodus covered forty years; the great tribulation will be only three and a half years. The pillar took them all the way to the crossing of the Jordan and the promised land. The pillar will be leading all the way to the resurrection and the promised kingdom.

One of the last events at Mount Sinai was the construction of the tabernacle, also called the tent of meeting. The appearance of the cloud is significantly stated then.

> *Then the cloud covered the tent of meeting, and the glory of the* Lord *filled the tabernacle. Moses was not able to enter the tent of meeting because the cloud had settled on it, and the glory of the* Lord *filled the tabernacle.*
> **Exodus 40:34-35**

# THE CLOUD BY DAY, THE FIRE BY NIGHT

Once the tabernacle was constructed, the cloud remained over the tabernacle. When the cloud moved, the tabernacle was disassembled and moved until the cloud came to rest. This entire description is given to us again in the Book of Numbers.

> *Now on the day that the tabernacle was erected the cloud covered the tabernacle, the tent of the testimony, and in the evening it was like the appearance of fire over the tabernacle, until morning. So it was continuously; the cloud would cover it by day, and the appearance of fire by night. Whenever the cloud was lifted from over the tent, afterward the sons of Israel would then set out; and in the place where the cloud settled down, there the sons of Israel would camp. At the command of the LORD the sons of Israel would set out, and at the command of the LORD they would camp; as long as the cloud settled over the tabernacle, they remained camped. Even when the cloud lingered over the tabernacle for many days, the sons of Israel would keep the LORD's charge and not set out. If sometimes the cloud remained a few days over the tabernacle, according to the command of the LORD they remained camped. Then according to the command of the LORD they set out. If sometimes the cloud remained from evening until morning, when the cloud was lifted in the morning, they would move out; or if it remained in the daytime and at night, whenever the cloud was lifted, they would set out. Whether it was two days or a month or a year that the cloud lingered over the tabernacle, staying above it, the sons of Israel remained camped and did not set out; but when it was lifted, they did set out.*
>
> **Numbers 9:15-22**

There are other Scriptures that note how God's presence was in the cloud. In fact, it is part of God's faithfulness to Israel to remain with them in the wilderness journey. Nehemiah said it this way in poetic fashion.

## THE CLOUD BY DAY, THE FIRE BY NIGHT

*You, in Your great compassion, did not forsake them in the wilderness; the pillar of cloud did not leave them by day, to guide them on their way, nor the pillar of fire by night, to light for them the way in which they were to go.*
**Nehemiah 9:19**

The pillar and the tabernacle became integral parts of the camp of Israel. Whenever issues arose, God would make His presence known in the cloud at the tabernacle, followed by God giving counsel to Moses. When the seventy elders of Israel were anointed to join Moses in leadership, the cloud was involved.

*Then the LORD came down in the cloud and spoke to him [Moses]; and He took of the Spirit who was upon him and placed Him [the Holy Spirit] upon the seventy elders. And when the Spirit rested upon them, they prophesied. But they did not do it again.* **Numbers 11:25**

When Miriam, Moses' sister, spoke against Moses, the LORD in the cloud corrected Miriam.

*⁵Then the LORD came down in a pillar of cloud and stood at the doorway of the tent, and He called Aaron and Miriam. When they had both come forward,. . . ¹⁰But when the cloud had withdrawn from over the tent, behold, Miriam was leprous, as white as snow. As Aaron turned toward Miriam, behold, she was leprous.* **Numbers 12:5, 10**

Again, at the rebellion of Korah the people rebelled against the LORD because of how He judged Korah.

*It came about, however, when the congregation had assembled against Moses and Aaron, that they turned toward the tent of meeting, and behold, the cloud covered it and the glory of the LORD appeared.* **Numbers 16:42**

The simple description of "the cloud covered it and the glory of the L_ORD_ appeared" does not convey the fear and awe that must have been present, but the instruction for the cloud of incense inside the sanctuary of the tabernacle certainly does.

> *²The L_ORD_ said to Moses, "Tell your brother Aaron that he shall not enter at any time into the holy place inside the veil, before the mercy seat which is on the ark, or he will die; for I will appear in the cloud over the mercy seat. ... ¹³He shall put the incense on the fire before the L_ORD_, that the cloud of incense may cover the mercy seat that is on the ark of the testimony, otherwise he will die."* **Leviticus 16:2, 13**

Maybe you have never thought of this before, but the cloud that led the children of Israel in the wilderness holds the very same power and essence of the very glory of God, which is inside the tabernacle, inside the Holy of Holies, with the cloud of incense above the mercy seat. While not explicitly written in Scripture, the traditional explanation given by the Jewish sages is that the smoke arising from the fire altar outside of the sanctuary was said to be a *pillar* as well. According to ancient temple testimony, the wind would **not** cause the smoke to drift and blow about, either in the sanctuary or from the temple altar in Jerusalem. It is said that the smoke rose straight up in the fashion of the pillar in the wilderness before dispersing into the air.

Let's shift gears to the New Testament Scriptures. Is there anything that compares to the events of the exodus and the tabernacle in the wilderness concerning the cloud? Knowing the pillar of cloud was God's presence in the camp, do we see events when a cloud represents God's presence in the days of the Messiah's ministry?

The answer is a resounding YES! Consider these events recorded in the Gospels. It wasn't as constant as with the exodus, but it did appear twice, bringing God the Father to speak of His Son.

## THE CLOUD BY DAY, THE FIRE BY NIGHT

The synoptic Gospels (Matthew, Mark, and Luke) all record the event of the transfiguration, when Yeshua appeared with Moses and Elijah before the disciples in a cloud.

> *While he was still speaking, behold, a bright cloud overshadowed them; and behold, a voice out of the cloud, said, "This is My beloved Son, with whom I am well-pleased; listen to Him!"* **Matthew 17:5**

> *Then a cloud formed, overshadowing them, and a voice came out of the cloud, "This is My beloved Son, listen to Him!"* **Mark 9:7**

> *While he was saying this, a cloud formed and began to overshadow them; and they were afraid as they entered the cloud. Then a voice came out of the cloud, saying, "This is My Son, My Chosen One; listen to Him!"* **Luke 9:34-35**

There is probably no more dramatic moment of Yeshua's presence with His disciples than this. It is comparable to Moses talking with the LORD in the cloud. This is similar to the dramatic observation that was reported to us when, forty days following His crucifixion, Yeshua departed from them and ascended into the cloud.

> *And after He [Yeshua] had said these things, He was lifted up while they were looking on, and a cloud received Him out of their sight.* **Acts 1:9**

It is clear from the testimony of the Tanach that the appearance of the *cloud by day and the fire by night* was the very presence of God—His glory, His power, and His majesty. The cloud was also part of Yeshua's presence when He came to do the work of redemption. The cloud is not just a thing of the past! The cloud has a future and it will be part of the *Greater Exodus* and the return of the Messiah.

## THE CLOUD BY DAY, THE FIRE BY NIGHT

The Apostle Paul refers to this future by reminding us of the lessons of the cloud in the past.

> *For I do not want you to be unaware, brethren, that our fathers were all under the cloud...* **1 Corinthians 10:1**

When the great tribulation comes and many brethren escape to the camps of the righteous as part of the *Greater Exodus*, the hope is that they will do much better than their forefathers did. The *cloud by day and a fire by night* will be in those camps. The prophet Isaiah says it will be part of the reason why the tribulation saints will escape, survive, and endure.

> *In that day the Branch of the LORD will be beautiful and glorious, and the fruit of the earth will be the pride and the adornment of the <u>survivors</u> of Israel. It will come about that <u>he who is left</u> in Zion and remains in Jerusalem will be called holy—<u>everyone who is recorded for life</u> in Jerusalem. When the Lord has washed away the filth of the daughters of Zion, and purged the bloodshed of Jerusalem from her midst, by the spirit of judgment and the spirit of burning, then the LORD will create over the whole area of Mount Zion and over her assemblies* [the camps of the righteous in the *Greater Exodus*] ***a cloud by day, even smoke, and the brightness of a flaming fire by night****; for over all the glory will be a canopy. There will be a shelter* [a sukkah] *to give shade from the heat by day, and refuge and protection from the storm and the rain.*
> **Isaiah 4:2-6**

This passage is not talking about the history of the exodus of Egypt; it is talking about the events at the end of the age as part of the great tribulation and the *Greater Exodus*. Let me share one last place from Isaiah that testifies to the pillar being in the camps during the great tribulation.

## THE CLOUD BY DAY, THE FIRE BY NIGHT

In the final months and days of the tribulation, darkness will cover the earth. It will be caused by a "deep impact" from an asteroid or comet. This is described in Revelation 8:12 and 9:1-2. But Isaiah says that the remnant will have light.

> *Arise, shine; for your light has come, and the glory of the LORD has risen upon you. For behold, darkness will cover the earth, and deep darkness the peoples; but the LORD will rise upon you, and His glory will appear upon you. Nations will come to your light, and kings to the brightness of your rising.* **Isaiah 60:1-3**

What is the source of light that they will have when the world is in darkness? Answer: the pillar of cloud by day fire by night.

Let us step back and consider what all this means. The saints will escape from their homes and cities, joining other brethren in their sukkahs (mobile shelters). God leads them from camping location to camping location with a *cloud by day and a pillar of fire by night*. The cloud will remind them daily of God's presence in every camp. The Messiah will truly lead them. Should the enemy approach, the cloud will most likely stand between the enemy and the saints. The Glory of God will be with them. The cloud will be a great canopy (sukkah) over them, shielding them from radiation and adverse weather elements. The stage will be set for the final event.

> *And then they will see the Son of Man coming in a cloud with power and great glory.* **Luke 21:27**

On that day, everyone (believer and unbeliever) will be compelled to take note of that cloud and the presence of the Messiah (Son of Man). That will be a glorious day because the cloud will shine very brightly!

## THE CLOUD BY DAY, THE FIRE BY NIGHT

*The light of the moon will be as the light of the sun, and the light of the sun will be seven times brighter, like the light of seven days, on the day the* L{\small ORD} *binds up the fracture of His people and heals the bruise He has inflicted.*

**Isaiah 30:26**

The *Greater Exodus* follows the pattern of the exodus out of Egypt. The Messiah as part of the Godhead was in the cloud; He led the children of Israel out of Egypt. He is the One who led them to the mountain and gave them His Instructions (the Torah). He is the One who builds the tabernacle in our hearts and inhabits it. He is the One who takes us to the promised land. The same cloud was there when the disciples heard the voice of the Father say, "*This is my beloved Son...*" It is the same cloud that Yeshua ascended to heaven in. It is the same cloud that we will see in the camps of the *Greater Exodus*. This is how the Messiah will lead us in all of the various camps and different nations to the promised land. It will be the same cloud that will bring Him back to rule and reign triumphantly from Jerusalem.

# FIFTEEN

# COMING FACE TO FACE WITH HIM

As I conclude the subject of this book, I have sought to accomplish two things: to lay a firm Scriptural foundation for the doctrine of the *Greater Exodus* and to address prophetic implications for the final generation that will see the coming of the LORD. I believe that Jeremiah was correct in emphasizing the greatness of the future exodus as compared with the ancient one.

From Moses to the Book of Revelation, the prophecies of the *Greater Exodus* are specific and detailed. The elements of the future exodus are interwoven in the historical exodus from Egypt. They are the inspiration for the Messiah to do greater things beyond the person of Moses. They both are joined together with the profound end-time events, including the restoration of the two Houses of Israel, the great tribulation, and the drama of the Book of Revelation.

If we are the final generation that will not pass away until all is fulfilled, as spoken of by Moses, then theses prophecies are more than an eschatology study to us. The *Greater Exodus* may well be our very own personal destiny, and we may be the very peoples tested and proved by God at the end. The question for us is simple. Will we do better than those who came out of Egypt, or will we fail for lack of faith, just like them? We should be able to do better since we have been given the knowledge of the past, the lessons to be learned, and the correct answers for each test, but will we complete the course?

Maybe I am overly optimistic, however, I am convinced that something wonderful will take place—that we will learn the lessons from the exodus and avoid the pitfalls of unbelief and complaining. I also believe that we are the last generation and will be part of the reason it will be called the *Greater Exodus*. One thing is certain, we don't have the personal or collective wisdom to pull this off on our own. God will have to pour out His Spirit on us all (just as He has promised to do) and we will need God's direction at a personal level. On this last point, let me take you back to one of the most direct prophecies given by Ezekiel.

> *...and I will bring you into the wilderness of the peoples, and there I will enter into judgment with you face to face.*
> **Ezekiel 20:35**

The phrase *"face to face"* is significant in comparison to the exodus. *Face to face* was the description of hearing God's voice at Mount Sinai.

> *The* LORD *spoke to you face to face at the mountain from the midst of the fire,...* **Deuteronomy 5:4**

The voice they heard was overwhelmingly awesome, with rocks splitting, trees shattering, and animals giving birth. According to Psalm 29, the voice of God is like thunder—like a thunder clap that immediately follows a flash of lightning. There is no delay. It is disturbing and almost terrorizing in the moment that it occurs. The children of Israel, standing at the base of Mount Sinai, thought they would die if they heard Him speak again. This is why the people requested Moses to ascend the mountain on their behalf and bring back God's words to them. God agreed to this and added that He would do the same with the Messiah—

## COMING FACE TO FACE WITH HIM

He would send the Messiah down from the mountain and speak the Word of God to us directly, just as a friend or brother would speak (Deuteronomy 18:15-16).

Once this agreement was in place, God did not speak with the people face to face anymore. Moses was left with that task, and we have the written word now for every generation to read.

> *Thus the* LORD *used to speak to Moses face to face, just as a man speaks to his friend...* **Exodus 33:11**

This is one of Moses' special attributes that makes him different from other prophets and men of God.

> *Since that time no prophet has risen in Israel like Moses, whom the* LORD *knew face to face,...* **Deuteronomy 34:10**

Today, we enjoy that agreement concerning whom God speaks with face to face. God does not speak from the mountain to us, scaring us half to death. Instead, we have the Torah (God's instructions given to Moses), and we have the same instructions that our ancestors received. Even further, we have received the promise that God made to Moses, and the Messiah has descended from the mountain to speak to us. We have enjoyed the very presence of the Messiah Himself and He has spoken to us like a friend, like God spoke to Moses. Additionally, we have received the Holy Spirit and can hear the small, quiet voice of God speaking to us in spiritual words and spiritual thoughts.

> *Now we have received, not the spirit of the world, but the Spirit who is from God, that we may know the things freely given to us by God, which things we also speak, not in words taught by human wisdom, but in those taught by the Spirit, combining spiritual thoughts with spiritual words.*
> **1 Corinthians 2:12-13**

However, when the prophecy of Ezekiel 20:35 says that God will speak with us face to face in the *Greater Exodus*, something much greater will take place. Will God speak with us again just as He did at Mount Sinai? Will we hear the voice of God? The answer is Yes. But this time He will speak from heaven and shake the entire Universe.

> *And His voice shook the earth then, but now He has promised, saying, "Yet once more I will shake not only the earth, but also the heaven."* **Hebrews 12:26**

The writer of Hebrews used this quote from the prophet Haggai, when the prophet was encouraging Zerubbabel to build the temple again in Jerusalem. He spoke of a time coming when God would speak again with His voice shaking the heavens and the earth. He spoke of that future time when many people would also come out of the nations and come to Jerusalem (the *Greater Exodus*).

> *⁵As for the promise which I made you when you came out of Egypt, My Spirit is abiding in your midst; do not fear! ⁶For thus says the LORD of hosts, "Once more in a little while, I am going to shake the heavens and the earth, the sea also and the dry land. ⁷I will shake all the nations; and they will come with the wealth of all nations, and I will fill this house with glory," says the LORD of hosts... ⁹"The latter glory of this house will be greater than the former," says the LORD of hosts, "and in this place I shall give peace," declares the LORD of hosts.*
> **Haggai 2:5-7, 9**

This also is when God will give us the seventh and final promised covenant—the covenant of Peace. It will be given to us at the conclusion of the great tribulation, the *day of the LORD*, and the *Greater Exodus*.

> *My servant David will be king over them, and they will all have one shepherd; and they will walk in My ordinances and keep My statutes and observe them. They will live on the land that I gave to Jacob My servant, in which your fathers lived; and they will live on it, they, and their sons, and their sons' sons, forever; and David My servant shall be their prince forever. I will make a **covenant of peace** with them; it will be an everlasting covenant with them. And I will place them and multiply them, and will set My sanctuary in their midst forever. My dwelling place also will be with them; and I will be their God, and they will be My people. And the nations will know that I am the LORD who sanctifies Israel, when My sanctuary is in their midst forever.* **Ezekiel 37:24-28**

The Book of Revelation also refers to God speaking from heaven during the great tribulation as the *Seven Thunders*. God will make seven pronouncements.

> *I saw another strong angel coming down out of heaven, clothed with a cloud; and the rainbow was upon his head, and his face was like the sun, and his feet like pillars of fire; and he had in his hand a little book which was open. He placed his right foot on the sea and his left on the land; and he cried out with a loud voice, as when a lion roars; and when he had cried out, the seven peals of thunder uttered their voices. When the seven peals of thunder had spoken, I was about to write; and I heard a voice from heaven saying, "Seal up the things which the seven peals of thunder have spoken, and do not write them."* **Revelation 10:1-4**

We do not know what God will say to us when He speaks in that day, but we do know He will speak again shaking the heavens. Whatever He says, we will experience the same *face to face* communication that our ancestors experienced at Mount Sinai.

## COMING FACE TO FACE WITH HIM

There is something more in the expression *face to face* given by Ezekiel that relates to the relationship Moses had face to face with God. Many of us are experienced in different levels of communication. We can write a letter, or send an e-mail, we have cell phones and text messaging. But, the most direct form of communication is still talking with someone face to face and actually seeing their face.

The Apostle John made reference to this in his epistles.

> *Though I have many things to write to you, I do not want to do so with paper and ink; but I hope to come to you and speak face to face, that your joy may be made full.*
> ***2 John 1:12***

Moses would go to the tent of meeting and speak to God while He was in the cloud. Even Moses didn't **see** God *face to face*; he **spoke** with God *face to face*. When Moses asked to see the face of God, he was told that he could not. Instead, God placed Moses in a cleft of a rock, limiting his view, and permitted him to see God's hand and then His back. This is when God wrote the second set of tablets of the Law for him. But the tribulation saints will experience something beyond Moses. As incredible as it may be, we are going to be transformed in such a way to permit us to see the face of God. It is mortals who cannot see God *face to face*, but if we have put on immortality (the final element of the *Greater Exodus*) then everything has changed. This may be the one outstanding element that truly makes it the **Greater Exodus**.

Those who traveled in the wilderness out of Egypt were transformed from slaves into free men, and the nation of Israel was formed. But those who travel in the *Greater Exodus* will be transformed from mortals of this world to immortals of God's kingdom. They will enter the true promised land and the Messianic Age.

## COMING FACE TO FACE WITH HIM

This transformation will eliminate all of our mortal concerns of life. Obeying the LORD will be the natural and normal thing to do, as common as inhaling and exhaling the air we breathe. God will not just be dealing with us in a corporate (group) manner; He will deal with each of us personally – *face to face*. The Apostle Peter has defined what we should be experiencing today (but we don't), but it definitely defines the days in the future for us.

> *Grace and peace be multiplied to you in the knowledge of God and of Yeshua our Lord; seeing that His divine power has granted to us everything pertaining to life and godliness, through the true knowledge of Him who called us by His own glory and excellence. For by these He has granted to us His precious and magnificent promises, in order that by them you might become partakers of the divine nature, having escaped the corruption that is in the world by lust. Now for this very reason also, applying all diligence, in your faith supply moral excellence, and in your moral excellence, knowledge; and in your knowledge, self-control, and in your self-control, perseverance, and in your perseverance, godliness; and in your godliness, brotherly kindness, and in your brotherly kindness, love. For if these qualities are yours and are increasing, they render you neither useless nor unfruitful in the true knowledge of our Lord Yeshua the Messiah. For he who lacks these qualities is blind or short-sighted, having forgotten his purification from his former sins. Therefore, brethren, be all the more diligent to make certain about His calling and choosing you; for as long as you practice these things, you will never stumble; for in this way the entrance into the eternal kingdom of our Lord and Savior Yeshua the Messiah will be abundantly supplied to you.* **2 Peter 1:2-11**

Or as the Apostle Paul said is our ultimate goal.

> ...*until we all attain to the unity of the faith, and of the knowledge of the Son of God, to a mature man, to the measure of the stature which belongs to the fullness of the Messiah.*
> *...but speaking the truth in love, we are to grow up in all aspects into Him, who is the head, even the Messiah, from whom the whole body, being fitted and held together by that which every joint supplies, according to the proper working of each individual part, causes the growth of the body for the building up of itself in love.* **Ephesians 4:13,15-16**

Let's be honest about our present walk before God. We are still in the nations awaiting the great outpouring of the Holy Spirit. We are babes and sucklings on the path toward spiritual maturity. We squabble with one another and behave like children who are hungry or not getting our way. Our idea of repentance is saying we are sorry and then repeating the same behavior we said we were sorry for. Our idea of making restitution and taking responsibility for our actions before the LORD is shallow at best. We are not prepared to follow the cloud, eat manna, drink water from a Rock, or hear God speak from heaven. Our own fears are the giants in the land persuading us to give up and go back to *Egypt*. There are not many (if any) Joshuas and Calebs among us.

Our generation is no better than the one which came out of Egypt in terms of spiritual maturity and wisdom. You would think that the redemption of the Messiah and the indwelling Holy Spirit would make us more prepared, but we are scattered in the nations and slaves to sin every bit as much as they were slaves in Egypt. How, then, are we to make this incredible transition and journey into the kingdom?

How will we pass the same tests of belief and obedience they faced? Will we have rebellion in the camp? Will we mumble and grumble against the leadership and the LORD? Will we reject the kingdom and ask to return to the world as our forefathers asked to return to Egypt?

If we are to have a different result from them, God will have to deal with us individually *face to face* and change our hearts one by one. This is what Ezekiel meant when he said God will deal with those traveling in the wilderness of the peoples *face to face*. This is the amazing part! According to the prophecies, God will be successful in working with us. At the completion of the *Greater Exodus*, we will be clothed in righteousness and see His face.

> *It was given to her* [the Bride of the Messiah] *to clothe herself in fine linen, bright and clean; for the fine linen is the righteous acts of the saints.* **Revelation 19:8**

> *For the* LORD *is righteous; He loves righteousness; the upright will behold His face.* **Psalm 11:7**

**COMING FACE TO FACE WITH HIM**

# A DIARY INTO THE FUTURE

*Passover Night*
We are excited. We have seen the altar shut down. The image of the antimessiah has been set up. The two witnesses are prophesying. We are eating the Passover with our "loins girded, sandals on, and staff in hand." My wife is joking that we don't need to clean the dishes tonight since we are leaving tomorrow. Ha. We are about to begin the journey of our lives. We are going on the *Greater Exodus*.

*10th day in the camp*
Various people are being sealed in the forehead. I don't know who is more shocked, us or them. People are asking if they can go back and get things they forgot. No one is being permitted to go. The Pillar has appeared. It is much bigger than I imagined. Everyone is amazed by the light at night.

*One month in the camp – 1220 days left in the great tribulation*
I am going to count the days to completion instead of how long we have been gone from our homes. We need to focus on where we are going, not what we left. We just completed our first move of the camp. It was incredible watching everyone with their stuff. I had to laugh. Some of them look like the Beverly Hillbillies. We went northward. With summer coming, I guess we are like the birds—north for the summer; south for the winter. Start-

ing to run out of food, the leadership is telling us that the manna will come soon.

*1203 days left*
Some people are getting restless. We are running short on water in the camp. Several of us are speaking with the leaders, and they are asking the Lord for the "springs of water" that He promised. I think it is a test to see if we will trust Him. A couple of people don't seem to be too trusting.

*1157 days left*
Today was weird. The Pillar suddenly spread out over the whole camp. Shortly thereafter, we heard helicopters flying over the camp. They went away and the Cloud formed again as a Pillar. I'm not sure what was happening but some of the guys thought it might be *Pharaoh's chariots* trying to find us. I was fishing at the time. I had grilled fish, salad greens, and manna hush puppies tonight.

*1132 days left*
The weather kicked up today with thunderstorms, lightning, and wind, but it didn't hit us. Everything seemed to move around us. We did get some rain; it washed everything off and we filled our containers. A bunch of people had fun dancing in the rain.

*1085 days left*
The season has definitively changed. It is cold in the evenings and the mornings. Need to get some more wood ready for my stove at night. Then my sukkah is nice and cozy.

*1012 days left*
There was a big meeting in the camp today. Several people were saying it would be better to go back to their homes. We were trying to convince them that leaving the camp would be death and their homes aren't there anymore. Some were arguing about

other things in the camp. All of this complaining is not good for anyone in the camp. I tried to explain that we have no reason to complain. We are safe right now. Let's just wait on the LORD. Besides, the LORD is definitely with us. He has not left us out here to die.

*992 days left*
We have moved again. More to the south this time. It is still cold at night but the Sun warms us up pretty good in the daytime. We went by some small towns, no one was there. We foraged what we could. Several of us gathered a bunch of wood. There was no food left in the town.

*975 days left*
We kept our first Passover in the wilderness. We made our own Matzah and ate real ground horseradish. It wasn't like any kind of store bought stuff either - the real thing - cleared my sinuses. I have planted my tomato seeds in a bucket today. I hope I can grow a few along the way.

*971 days left*
Some scavengers showed up last evening about sundown. There was no question that they were scoping us out. I hope they just move on. The leaders are forming up a group to watch the perimeter better. Some of the leaders were able to buy a couple head of cattle (they would only take gold or silver). They were butchered so everyone could have meat in their camp sites for the next couple of days. My neighbor has a goat on a tether. I keep teasing him by calling his goat "Sunday Brunch."

*960 days left*
It finally happened. A group of about 20 bad guys hit the edge of the camp. They were like animals. We are okay. They all died. One of the "sealed ones" got shot. It knocked him down, but he just got right back up. There was not a mark on him. Everyone

was told to camp closer to the main group and not to set up away from the main group.

*927 days left*
I'm not sure how many times we have moved the camp now. Each move is running into the next one. I lost some of my equipment, must have left it back there. The sky is really dirty. You can smell smoke everywhere, and the sun and moon are giving off weird colors, different shades of orange.

*845 days left*
My camping neighbor got upset with me today and moved his camp away from me. I didn't mean to upset him. While some are settled in the routine, others get easily offended. It's probably the stress and the routine. My other neighbor just brought me a new recipe for preparing manna. Who would've guessed that it makes great dough for pizza. I made the sauce with my "bucket tomatoes" and topped it off with "goat cheese." The only thing missing was a cold beer.

*816 days left*
Strangers came by the camp today. They wanted to join us but they weren't believers. They have taken the implant (the mark) and now have a severe sore at that location. They did tell us that a lot of people have died in the big cities. They have food in the cities, if that is what you call it, but everyone is sick and there is no more medicine. They said that one cannot leave the cities and travel to the next unless it is official government business. But they escaped and figured they would be better off outside of the city. You can tell that they are very desperate and probably dangerous to us.

*749 days left*
The routine in the camp is getting old. Every day I have to get more water and fuel for the stove. I try to keep busy with small

things but it's mostly "hurry up and wait." Many of us get together in the evening to talk, read Scripture, and pray. This whole experience is very humbling. You look around and can see people changing. We are all losing weight; some of my clothes are baggy now. Some of the women have offered to make some alterations and re-sew them for me.

*645 days left*
We are halfway through the great tribulation. Messiah Yeshua was not kidding when He said it would be a "Great" tribulation. We have heard rumors about different judgments but I keep referring to the Book of Revelation for what is really happening.

*500 days left*
You would think that there would be no rebels in this camp any longer. Wrong! Several families left the camp today. Some people just don't know when they have it good. They think they know better than everyone else and the LORD. A lot of people were crying when they left. Maybe we will see them in the kingdom.

*430 days left*
I am not getting used to this… it is a struggle, but the days seem to be getting shorter. At least, we keep counting them off. I like this particular campsite. There aren't any more trees to speak of and the grass is gone, but I sense God is with us in the camp. The Pillar is still there; I like the shade from it. We prayed for some sick folks today, they are well now.

*355 days left*
We discovered another camp of believers. Actually, the Pillar led us to another camp and we have joined them making the new camp even larger. The two pillars became one. That was interesting to watch. We now have lots of new folks to meet and get to know. They sure were excited to see us. They thought they were the last people in the world.

*135 days left*
The darkness is here. The sky is full of dark clouds. You can tell it is ash and dust, there is a light coating of it on everything. The pillar of light reflects off the sky and it makes the sky look like it is made of bronze or iron. There is definitely no sun or moon to see.

*99 days left*
The locust demons came by us but were ordered away by the sealed ones. That was good, because they are big and ugly. I admit it. I was freaked out. If the sealed ones had not been here I don't know what we would have done.

*7 days left*
The anticipation of what is next is all through the camp. Everyone is telling one another "We are going to make it!" There is no question anymore. God has saved us if the tribulation does really end. Some people are crying but they are crying with joy and relief. I will be so glad to be out of this darkness; it is so gloomy. I don't know what we would do without the pillar of fire above us.

*5 days after the end of the tribulation*
We just finished gathering for prayer and everyone is repenting. I have never before seen a group of people so humble and contrite. We are counting the days to Yom Teruah (when we get our new bodies). Just 25 days until Trumpets!

*15 days after the end of the tribulation*
I'm still shaking. We just heard God's voice come from the sky (heaven)? He just announced seven judgments on the world. So, this is what it was like back at Mount Sinai? I feel so weak. The overcast of clouds is starting to break up. We can see light rays streaming down from between the clouds and hitting the earth. It is almost surreal. The light is very bright. I guess we have been in the darkness so long that our eyes are sensitive to that much light.

*21 days after the end of the tribulation*
We have now seen the light. It wasn't the sun. We have seen the sign of the Son of Man in the clouds of heaven! The clouds are rolling back now and it is hard to look at Him. He is so bright. Needless to say, everyone in the camp is rejoicing and dancing around. Some people are just staring up at Him. I even danced today! It won't be long now. Everyone is blowing their shofars in the camp and every time we hear one, everyone thinks it's "resurrection" and then we all start laughing at each other's reactions when we are still here. When God's shofar from heaven is sounded, I won't even try to make a diary entry. I probably won't be able to.

*45 days after the End of the Tribulation - In Jerusalem*
The number of people is unbelievable. Everyone is laughing and crying with joy. We are seeing and meeting people that were resurrected. I'm with my Grandpa and Grandma and others in my family. It was just like He said, we heard the shofar, people came up from everywhere, then suddenly I was with them. All of my aches and pains are gone – my new body! We went up in the clouds and looked down on the earth. We were flying like clouds. We could hear everything on the ground. Then God's judgment hit. I have never seen so much lightning or heard so many sounds. The fire of God was blue and red, and gold, and everywhere. The ground of the earth was shaking like a sieve and everything was shaken. We were flying here several days and have just arrived. Jerusalem and the surrounding area is a lot different from what I remember. God has made some big changes to everything. We floated back to the ground and we are watching the area of the Mount of Olives. We have our palm branches ready to make a sukkah. I'm an expert at that now. The King of Righteousness will be here very soon. I hope I can finally see Him today.

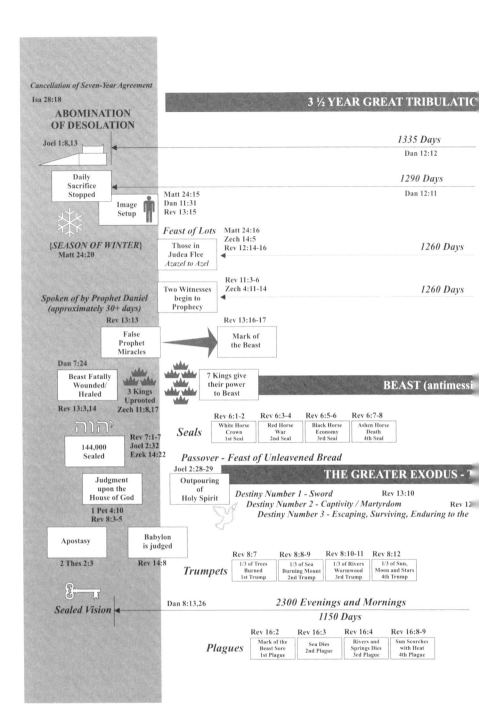

# Tribulation Timeline
## (a time, times, and half a time)

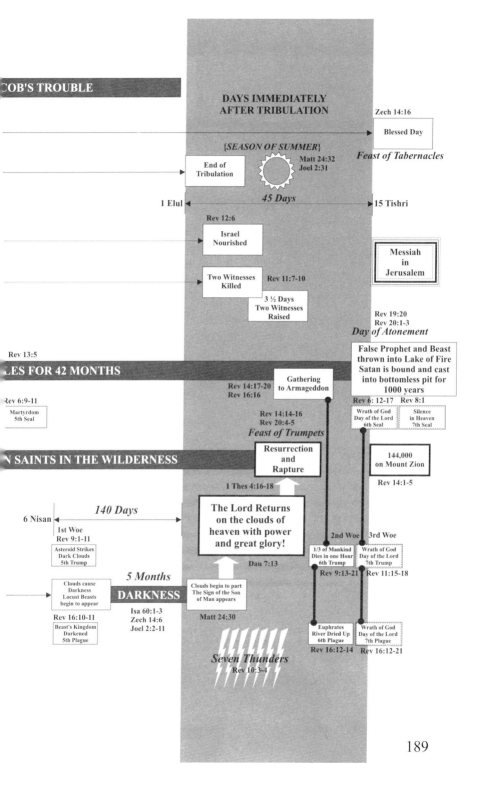

# INDEX OF SCRIPTURES

Scripture References Used in this Book

Scriptures taken from the NEW AMERICAN STANDARD BIBLE®, © 1960, 1962, 1963, 1968, 1971, 1972, 1973, 1975, 1977, 1995 by The Lockman Foundation. Used by permission.

Dedication
    Joshua 1:5-7, 9

Chapter 1 - God Planned the First Exodus

    Genesis 15:2
    Genesis 15:13-16
    Exodus 12:41
    Exodus 6:6-8
    Deuteronomy 8:3-5
    Deuteronomy 8:6-10

Chapter 2 - God has Planned for Another Exodus

    Isaiah 46:8-11
    Isaiah 46:11
    Jeremiah 16:14-15
    Jeremiah 23:5-8
    Jeremiah 29:11-14
    Deuteronomy 4:27-31
    Deuteronomy 32

Chapter 3 - How Does God Save All Israel?

    Romans 3:31
    Genesis 12:3

Galatians 3:8
Romans 9:6
Romans 9:8
Romans 11:17-18
Jeremiah 5:10
Jeremiah 11:16
Romans 11:17-18
Romans 11:25-28
Isaiah 2:2-3
Psalm 14:7
Psalm 53:6
Isaiah 46:12-13
1 Corinthians 10:1-11

Chapter 4 - Having Eyes to See and Ears to Hear

Deuteronomy 29:10
Deuteronomy 29:22
Matthew 24:34
Deuteronomy 29:28
Leviticus 26:27, 33, 38
Leviticus 26: 44-45
Deuteronomy 30:1-10
Deuteronomy 29:2-5
Isaiah 64:1-4
1 Corinthians 2:9-10
Ezekiel 39:29
Isaiah 8:20
John 5:47
Deuteronomy 30:1-10
Deuteronomy 31:8
Deuteronomy 32
Revelation 15:3
Isaiah 66:19-22

Chapter 5 - Why Judaism Believes in the Greater Exodus

    Genesis 15:16
    Jeremiah 29:10
    2 Chronicles 36:20-21
    Deuteronomy 18:18-19
    Isaiah 49:1-4
    Matthew 1:20-21
    Luke 2:25-26
    Luke 2:36-38
    Isaiah 52:7-10
    Luke 2:29-30
    Isaiah 52:11-12
    Exodus 3:7
    Isaiah 49:14-15
    Isaiah 49:24-26
    Isaiah 50:1-3

Chapter 6 - Ending the Exile and Working toward Restoration

    Ezekiel 39:23-24
    Ezekiel 39:25-27
    Isaiah 49:5-7
    Isaiah 49:8-13
    Joshua 5:13-15
    Matthew 3:13-15
    Exodus 19:10
    1 Corinthians 10:1-2
    Jeremiah 31:31-32
    Isaiah 9:1
    Luke 4:17-21
    Isaiah 61:1-2a
    John 1:46
    Isaiah 61:2b-3
    Isaiah 61:7

Isaiah 61:10
Matthew 4:13-16
John 10:14-16
Jeremiah 23:3-5
Jeremiah 23:7-8
Jeremiah 16:14-15
Romans 9:8
Romans 11
Matthew 10:5-6

Chapter 7 - The Great Tribulation and the Greater Exodus

Matthew 24:21
Zephaniah 1:14-18
Isaiah 13:6-13
Zephaniah 2:1-3
Zephaniah 3:14-20
Isaiah 10:20-23
Isaiah 11:11-16
Isaiah 34:8
Joel 1:15
Joel 2:1
Joel 2:30-32
Daniel 12:1b
Revelation 6:8
Revelation 9:18
Ezekiel 14:13-14
Ezekiel 14:16
Ezekiel 14:20
Ezekiel 14:21
Ezekiel 14:22-23

Chapter 8 - Who is Able to Stand in that Day?

    Revelation 6:17
    Revelation 7:4
    Ezekiel 37:1-6
    Ezekiel 36:24, 26-28
    Ezekiel 37:16-19
    Ezekiel 37:20-23
    Zechariah 11:14
    Revelation 14:1
    Numbers 31:48-49
    Revelation 7:9-10
    John 7:37
    Zechariah 14:16
    Revelation 7:14b-17
    Isaiah 49:10
    Deuteronomy 8:2-3
    Revelation 2:17b
    Psalm 91:5-10
    Ezekiel 20:33-38
    Revelation 11:3-6
    Revelation 12:1-6
    Zechariah 14:5
    Matthew 24:15-16, 20-21
    Revelation 12:13-17
    Deuteronomy 32:11
    Revelation 14:14-19

Chapter 9 - Comparing the Future with the Ancient Past

    Jeremiah 30:7
    Isaiah 46:9-11
    Jeremiah 16:14-16
    Genesis 48:16
    Genesis 48:19

Deuteronomy 33:17
Jeremiah 16:10-13
Jeremiah 16:17-21
Ezekiel 20:33-38
Jeremiah 32:21
Exodus 6:6
Deuteronomy 5:15a
Deuteronomy 7:19
Deuteronomy 9:29
Deuteronomy 11:2
Deuteronomy 26:8
1 Kings 8:42
1 Corinthians 15:51-52
1 Thessalonians 4:13-18
Ezekiel 20:36
Ezekiel 20:37-38
Revelation 11:5
Matthew 10:23b
Isaiah 4:5-6
Exodus 17:16
Deuteronomy 25:17-19
Number 16:1-35
Ezekiel 20:38
1 Corinthians 10:1-13

Chapter 10 - How Judaism Prepares for the Greater Exodus

Ezekiel 36:16-38
Jeremiah 16:10-13
Jeremiah 16:14-15
Ezekiel 36:22-32
Ezekiel 45:16 – 46:18
Ezekiel 45:21-24
Matthew 26:29
Malachi 3:4 – 4:4

Malachi 4:4-6
Deuteronomy 29:29
Genesis 37:12-13
Isaiah 10:32 – 12:6
Isaiah 11:11-13, 16

Chapter 11 - How Messianics Prepare for the Greater Exodus

Leviticus 23:39-43
Leviticus 23:34-36
Revelation 7:9
Leviticus 23:39-43
Exodus 23:16
Zechariah 14:16
Amos 9:11, 13-15
Acts 15:16-18
Hosea 1:10-11
Leviticus 26:27-45
Deuteronomy 32:47a

Chapter 12 - The Two Houses of Israel in the Greater Exodus

Jeremiah 30:3-7
Ezekiel 37:1-10
Zechariah 12:2-7
Ezekiel 37:11-23
Acts 15:22-29
Numbers 15:15-16
Luke 19:10
Matthew 15:24
Matthew 10:6
Hosea 1:10-11
Matthew 16:16
Ezekiel 39:21-29
Isaiah 11:13

Chapter 13 - Transitioning to Tribes in the Camps

    Exodus 14:11-14
    Exodus 14:30
    Exodus 16:3
    Exodus 16:15
    Exodus 16:29
    Exodus 17:7
    Exodus 18:21
    Exodus 18:25
    Numbers 1:4-16
    Exodus 13:18
    Revelation 7:1-3
    Ezekiel 9:2-4, 11
    Revelation 7:3-4
    Ezekiel 9
    Revelation 7:5-8
    Numbers 7:11-12
    Revelations 2:17
    Numbers 16:1-35

Chapter 14 - The Cloud by Day, the Fire by Night

    Exodus 13:20-22
    Exodus 14:19-20
    Exodus 14:24
    Exodus 16:10-15
    Exodus 19:9
    Exodus 40:34-38
    Numbers 9:15-22
    Nehemiah 9:19
    Numbers 11:25
    Numbers 12: 5, 10
    Numbers 16:42
    Leviticus 16:2, 13

Matthew 17:5
Mark 9:7
Luke 9:34-35
Acts 1:9
1 Corinthians 10:1
Isaiah 4:2-6
Revelation 8:12
Revelation 9:1-2
Isaiah 60:1-3
Luke 21:27
Isaiah 30:26

Chapter 15 - Coming Face to Face with Him

Ezekiel 20:35
Deuteronomy 5:4
Psalm 29
Deuteronomy 18:15-16
Exodus 33:11
Deuteronomy 34:10
1 Corinthians 2:12-13
Ezekiel 20:35
Hebrews 12:26
Haggai 2:5-7, 9
Ezekiel 37:24-28
Revelation 10:1-4
2 John 1:12
2 Peter 1:2-11
Ephesians 4: 13, 15-16
Revelation 19:8
Psalm 11:7

**FOR MORE TEACHINGS AND RESOURSES FROM MONTE JUDAH CONTACT:**

*Lion and Lamb Ministries*
P.O. Box 720968
Norman, Ok 73070

Phone: (405) 447-4429
Fax: (405) 447-3775
Web: www.lionlamb.net
E-mail: info@lionlamb.net

# THE GREATER EXODUS

## MONTE W. JUDAH

AUDIO BOOK

6 Audio CDs  -  **$45** Plus Shipping

*Available through Lion and Lamb Ministries*
www.lionlamb.net

# TRIBULATION HANDBOOK

Lion and Lamb Ministries has taught for many years that keeping the Feast of Tabernacles prepares you and your family to be a part of the Greater Exodus. Now, after keeping the Feast for many years with many brethren in the camp, we are publishing a Tribulation Handbook. This weatherproof handbook covers a whole range of lessons learned from keeping the Feast of Tabernacles! You don't want to go into the "camp of the righteous" in "the wilderness of the peoples" during the Great Tribulation without this handbook. It is a guide for your family and other likeminded brethren about how to set up the camp tailored to the threats of the Great Tribulation. It offers practical tips addressing survival and endurance issues. It offers spiritual counsel and encouragement to maintain trust in the Lord. Addendums in the handbook include: scriptural timelines for the Great Tribulation, the prophetic pattern of Numbers 33 (the 42 camping locations), packing lists to get ready, and songs for the Tribulation saints. This handbook is not a survival manual or wilderness guide, but it works hand in glove with those resources and addresses how to escape, survive, and endure the Great Tribulation. This handbook is flexible, weatherproof, and sized at 6"x9"x1" to fit in your Go-Bag.

108 Pages - **$29** Plus Shipping

*Available through Lion and Lamb Ministries*
*www.lionlamb.net*

This book has given me a much greater understanding on the Great Tribulation, and understanding the plan of God for His people.
*David Loredo*

Although Monte Judah has taught the subject for many years, it has never been compiled into one source before, which I hope will be of great service—and comfort—to Messianic believers and Christians as well.
*Jane Greene*

I was surprised to see so many Scriptures that are about the Greater Exodus.
*Lorne Greene*

Monte does a sensational job of explaining the Greater Exodus. This book will revolutionize your understanding of Bible prophecy and change your life. A MUST read!
*Eddie Chumney, Hebraic Heritage Ministries Int'l*

From the very first pages I was almost holding my breath. This is the story of the ages. It is so full of life-giving truths and encouragement that I found myself wanting to hurry-up and complete it so I could begin reading it again and again!
*Rosemary Burke*

Monte Judah has been blessed with an understanding of the Greater Exodus, and now, after many years of study, he is showing us a grand picture of the Greater Exodus.
*David Addington*